Developing Parenting Skills Confidence and Self-esteem

a training programme
by

Barbara Quartey & Tina Rae
illustrated by
Tina Rae

SAGE Publications Ltd
1 Oliver's Yard
55 City Road
London EC1Y 1SP

SAGE Publications Inc
2455 Teller Road
Thousand Oaks
California 91320

SAGE Publications India Pvt. Ltd
B 1/I 1 Mohan Cooperative Industrial Area
Mathura Road, New Delhi 110 044
India

SAGE Publications Asia-Pacific Pte Ltd
33 Pekin Street #02-01
Far East Square
Singapore 048763

Library of Congress Control Number available

British Library Cataloguing in Publication date

A catalogue record for this book is available from the British Library

ISBN-13 978-1-87394-268-0

Printed and bound in Great Britain by Cpod, Trowbridge, Wiltshire

Contents

How to use the CD-ROM

The CD-ROM contains a PDF file labelled 'Worksheets.pdf' which contains all the worksheets for each session in this resource. You will need Acrobat Reader version 3 or higher to view and print these resources.

The document is set up to print to A4 but you can enlarge the pages to A3 by increasing the output percentage at the point of printing using the page set-up settings for your printer.

Alternatively, you can photocopy the worksheets directly from this book at 100% on any A4 photocopier.

Biographical Notes

Tina Rae

B.A. (Hons) P.G.C.E. M.A.(Ed.) A.L.C.M. R.S.A.Dip.SplD. Dip.Psych (Open)

Tina Rae has taught in a range of different settings and contexts over the last 15 years including nursery, primary and high schools, music, art and drama workshops and in a special needs support service.

She worked as a SENCO prior to taking up her current post as Lead Teacher for pupils with Emotional and Behavioural Difficulties (EBD) in 1996.

Tina is committed to the inclusion of pupils and students with EBD and her work on emotional literacy and positive self-esteem is a reflection of this. Current publications for Lucky Duck Publishing include 'Dealing with Feeling' an emotional literacy curriculum for KS2 (1998), 'Crucial Skills' an anger management and problem solving course for high school students (1999), 'Positive People' self-esteem building for KS1 & 2 (2000), the CAS course (confidence, assertiveness and self-esteem building) for high school students (2000), 'Purr-fect Skills' a social and emotional skills training programme for KS1 (2000) and 'Coping with Change' (2000) for Folens Publishing.

Since the publication of these programmes and resources Tina has become a popular writer and speaker and continues to both collaborate with colleagues and work independently in order to produce exciting, attractive and practical packages for young people.

Tina is currently working with colleagues on a literacy programme for KS1 & 2 which enables teachers to teach the literacy hour and PSHE simultaneously. She is also preparing a series of 6 books to cover the PSHE and Citizenship curriculum for KS1 & 2.

This publication is the result of collaboration with Barbara Quartey and the resources have been successfully trialled with groups of parents whose children have a wide range of special educational needs.

Barbara Quartey

Bsc Hons PGCE MA.(Ed.)Management, Cert. Counselling

Barbara Quartey has worked in a number of educational and therapeutic settings over the past 18 years, including community and adult education, schools, nurseries, education and training advice, and youth counselling services.

She was Head of Department for basic education and science, a senior manager for community education and has lectured in Psychology, Sociology, Child Development and Education.

Barbara has also gained considerable expertise in the field of training in education, notably in delivering training on SEN issues to teachers in both special and mainstream schools and for school governors, nursery assistants and SEN support staff, and SMSA'S (school meals support assistants).

She has also run courses for social services departments and voluntary organisations, and has a particular interest in the area of team building and collegiate management systems.

Barbara is currently a Parent Partnership Coordinator and is committed to promote the recognition and inclusion of parents in the education of children. In her present post she develops and delivers training for Independent Parental Supporters, Mentors, school staff and Governors on working in partnership with parents in promoting the achievement of pupils.

Introduction and Background

This programme has been designed for use with parents/carers who would like to improve their relationship with their children and have a better understanding of challenging behaviour. The importance of the relationship between parents and children is central to this course.

The task for parents in the new millennium is possibly even harder than it has been for parents before them. Parents are more likely to be faced with a number of issues which they themselves did not experience as children such as developments in technology, concerns for safety of children and access to global information through the media.

"Bringing up children is perhaps the most challenging and important task that most of us perform and how well we do it is likely to have a continuing impact on future generations, playing a significant part in shaping the values and attitudes that young people take into their own adult relationships, and their approach to being a parent." (Pugh, De'Ath & Smith, 1994 p.9)

In many communities the extended family is less likely to be available to provide support, advice and help. The pressures on parents tend to be greater as more people are bringing up families as lone parents or in restructured families. Many parents are also in full or part-time employment and have to juggle commitments between home and work, which can cause additional pressures and stress within the family.

Parenting today is much more than just a set of skills, that are learnt through 'training' or classes. It is vital to raise awareness about the importance of the parenting role and how this involves understanding relationships, communication skills, social skills, practical skills and the incorporation of the emotional needs of all family members.

Many parents may feel and express negative thoughts about their children which are consequently transferred into negative actions. Alongside this can be the presumption that their children also hold a negative view of them as parents. This negative cycle may often appear impossible to break free from and is generally perpetuated by a range of social, economic and emotional factors. However, Goleman (1995), in his book 'Emotional Intelligence' reinforces the fact that parents can and do make a very real difference to the emotional health of their children. The quality and quantity of such a contribution is doubtlessly linked to levels of self-esteem, confidence and emotional literacy within both parents and children themselves. Consequently, these series of sessions aim to promote the self-esteem and confidence of parents. They are also intended to provide opportunities for the development of; practical skills, strategies and an emotional vocabulary with which to discuss and describe their relationships and responses.

Recent research (Rutter 1991, Goleman 1995) has emphasised the need to further enhance and develop self-esteem and identify the ways in which both schools as institutions with parents as key carers can help children develop the social skills and positive self-image necessary for managing themselves effectively in a range of social contexts. To enable parents to promote self-esteem in their children, they need to be given the opportunity to assess and evaluate their own skills and experiences in this area, asking questions such as; how do I cope in social situations? Do I receive appropriate levels of reinforcement and praise? If not, how can I change the situation and how can I ensure that both my child and I feel loved, worthwhile, appreciated and valued?

The course offers parents of children of all ages an opportunity to evaluate and reflect on both their own and their children's levels of self-esteem and confidence. It also enables them to identify their models and influences and as part of a supportive group develop a range of positive strategies for coping more effectively as a parent. Brief therapy techniques (George, Iveson and Ratner 1990) are used to support parents in the process of reflection, change and skills development.

Participants will have come to the group for a variety of reasons. Some will simply want to have time for themselves and a break from children, domestic chores, worries at home, work or about being unemployed. Others may want to increase their personal self-esteem, gain confidence, make friends and get support from other parents in similar situations. Some may just want to increase their understanding of children's development and how they can be more effective as parents.

Some participants may also bring with them psychological blocks such as:
  * A negative experience of failure from schooling.
  * Feeling of isolation, low self-esteem and lack of confidence in social groups.
  * Difficulties with literacy and self-expression.
  * English being a recently acquired language.
  * Feeling a failure as a parent because of other people's attitudes towards their
    children's behaviour.

All these may seem daunting, but it is not as challenging as it sounds. Participants will also share a number of similarities, the most obvious, their role as a parent. They will also have been a member of a family group, unit or other form of nurturing environment. It is also likely that participants will share the expectation that the group will offer them support, some level of friendship, as well as information which will provide a basis for group development and identity.

The facilitator will need to start from the participant's, experiences, values, personalities and motivation. They will also need to consider how to build on the knowledge and skills of group members whilst respecting individual, developmental needs and learning styles.

An empowering approach
This series of sessions has been designed to empower, motivate and enable parents to develop strategies within the context of a supportive, non-judgemental and non-threatening environment. Parents are encouraged to clarify and articulate their existing skills and strengths and to build upon these whilst gaining a greater understanding of the relationship(s) that they have with their children.

Course facilitators need to provide an environment in which participants feel safe in terms of expressing their views, feelings and experiences. For this reason, many of the activities have been designed to encourage working in small groups. Participants are also encouraged to change round the groups for each exercise so that they have an opportunity to work with different people. This process should help to break down any barriers within the group and enable the participants to benefit from the ideas and opinions of all participants and gain a broader perspective on issues and topics.

The importance of gaining a broader perspective is an important part of the empowering process. Participants should be encouraged to share belief systems, values and strategies on the central understanding that each member of the group will have something positive and worthwhile to offer (whether facilitator or participant) and that no one person can be or is the ultimate 'expert'.

The role of facilitator

Facilitator should be aware that the term parenting skills can cause unnecessary concern for some individuals who may be anxious about disclosing personal information about themselves and their family. This is not the case in this programme as any information that is disclosed is done so on a voluntary basis and at the discretion of each participant.

The facilitator will also need to be aware that developing self-awareness and confidence in parenting requires an environment in which participants feel able to discuss personal issues. It is therefore important that the environment reflects this i.e. the room is private, seating is comfortable and arranged so that whole group discussions as well as small groups work can take place.

The facilitators should also ensure that participants are provided with refreshments i.e. tea, coffee, light snacks as these 'comforts' help create a nurturing environment which helps facilitate learning.

Parenting skills programmes usually need a serious but light-hearted approach. The activities in this pack are designed to focus on skills in a supportive and non-threatening manner. It is therefore important that the facilitator is sensitive to the feelings and concerns of participants so that group members are not caused personal embarrassment or damage.

Ideally, the facilitator will have had some training in group facilitation, counselling or have considered the issues concerning parents in some depth. The manner in which any parenting skills programme is facilitated is critical to the success of the programme. The skills and personal qualities introduced to the participants should be clearly and sensitively modelled by the facilitator.

These include:
* Treating all participants with respect.
* Respecting confidences within and outside the sessions.
* Being non-judgemental.
* Self-awareness of own values, beliefs, attitudes and principles.
* Avoiding prescriptive or directive behaviour, allowing participants to help themselves or other group members.

* Realising personal limitations.
* Being honest and open to all opinions and views.
* Not presenting as the expert or giving more weight to your views.

Additional information to assist the facilitator in running the activities successfully and ethically is given within the session plans as and when appropriate. It is important to follow these guidelines so as to avoid unnecessary discomfort within the group.

How do you see your role?

How do you see your role as the group facilitator? This is an important question that all groups facilitators should consider, as the way in which facilitators perceive their role will be reflected in the manner in which they facilitate the group. The beliefs facilitators hold about how people learn, modify and change their behaviour will affect the kinds of experiences and opportunities they offer group participants.

It is important that facilitators are aware of the way in which they work with groups and know their own strengths and limitations. It is also vital that facilitators are flexible and responsive to the changing needs of the group and individual members. Facilitators should be able to maintain a balance between the individual needs of participants, the requirements of the group, and the activities or tasks to be covered. It may be useful for facilitators to consider their own attitudes, experiences, skills and support resources with reference to the following check list, prior to delivering the course.

Checklist

Attitudes:
* I am interested in people and I enjoy running groups.
* I don't feel the need to be in control all the time.
* I am flexible and willing to learn from group members.
* I enjoy informal open discussions.
* I am committed to supporting people's personal growth.
* I believe in people's ability to change.
* I am willing to look at and accept challenges about my own values and beliefs.
* I am committed in helping people to reach their own informed decisions.
* I believe that all parents would like to be 'good' parents, however some may need support.

Experiences:
* I have been a group member of an adult group.
* I have some experience of running groups for adults.
* I have had some basic training in group work.
* I have personal experiences that are especially relevant for this programme.

Skills:
* I am a good listener and I am aware of the things that I find painful to hear.
* I am reasonably confident about running a group.
* I know when I am under stress and can ask for support.

* I am able to adapt previously planned exercises to meet the needs of the group.
* I can manage the important boundaries, particularly those around confidentiality.
* I have skills in giving feedback and reflecting back to group members.
* I am prepared to acknowledge and deal with conflict.
* I am able to follow the programme pack and deliver the activity material.
* I am able to deal with both positive and negative emotions that may be expressed by the group.

Support resources:
* I have a network of people from whom I can seek information for group members.
* I have support for referring problems that are outside my scope.
* I have support for my own professional development.
* I have a co-leader with whom I can discuss key issues.

(Adapted from Confident Parents Confident Children. Pugh et al (1994)

Prospective facilitators may not be able to identify all of the above listed attitudes, experiences, skills and support resources, but may, on further reflection, feel that they have enough skills and personal resources to still deliver this programme. Through the process of delivering these sessions, the facilitators will be encouraged to develop their own skills, resources and learning style. Continual self-reflection is clearly the key to this process. However, we would not recommend that this course is delivered, in part or whole by any individual who has not received some basic training or has personal experience of group work.

Objectives
The sessions in this programme have been designed to meet the following objectives:
* To increase the self-esteem / self-concept of parents/carers and their children.
* To increase parents' beliefs in their own abilities as a parent/carer.
* To enable parents to reflect upon and develop their own skills, beliefs and strategies within a positive, supportive and constructive framework.
* To allow parents to identify and articulate their own models and influences and to be able to place these within the present context.
* To identify the characteristics of 'positive' parenting.
* To encourage the development of a network of support for parents.
* To improve parents' understanding of their children's behaviours and responses and their ability to accurately describe these behaviours.
* To be able to identify and label emotional triggers in oneself and one's children.
* To enable parents to identify potential conflict situations and to further develop personal strategies with which to cope more effectively.
* To encourage parents to identify strategies to increase their child(ren)'s self-esteem, confidence and ability to cope appropriately with conflict.
* To identify when and why parents need to both listen and talk to their children.
* To encourage parents to identify the signs which may lead to a conflict, emotionally charged situation and the consequent problem behaviours.
* To further develop real empathy for others.
* For parents to identify and explore a range of personal strategies to cope with difficult behaviour and conflict situations.
* To encourage parents to make use of brief therapy approaches in order to measure, evaluate and affect change.
* To enable parents to consider the concept of responsibility and ways in which they can encourage responsibility within their child(ren) i.e. for them to accept the consequences of their behaviours and actions.

* To encourage parents to work in partnership with the school(s) in terms of developing a consistent and agreed approach to discipline and behaviour.
* For parents to accept and appreciate themselves as agents of change.
* To promote and encourage the process of active listening and reflection.
* To promote the notion of a positive parent as opposed to a perfect parent.

Structure of the programme

The programme is arranged in 10 sessions as follows:

Session 1: Your self-esteem
* Agreement of group rules.
* Defining good self-esteem and completion of the self-esteem quick-quiz.
* Making use of a scaling activity to identify personal goals and targets.

Session 2: Your models and influences
* Identifying major models and influences on parenting styles.
* Articulating the characteristics of a positive parent.

Session 3: Managing emotions
* Identifying triggers to positive and negative feelings.
* Reflecting upon how we make others feel i.e. developing empathy.
* Articulating and identifying strategies to cope more effectively with anger.

Session 4: Children's self-esteem
* Identifying the self-esteem levels of children.
* Ways in which parents can further promote a positive self-image.

Session 5: Listening and talking
* Understanding when and why parents need to both listen and talk to their children.
* Tips for developing active listening skills and top ten quiz which enables parents to rate their own skills and to elicit children's views and opinions.

Session 6: Managing unacceptable behaviour
* Labelling and describing unacceptable behaviour and questioning the extent to which participants may or may not share social and family values and beliefs.
* Focusing on how children can learn from the consequences of their own behaviours.
* Discussion/reflection upon the do's and don'ts of discipline.

Session 7: Your child's responsibilities
* Identifying how and when children can take on responsibilities.
* Clarifying and agreeing characteristics of a responsible parent.
* Reflecting upon your own child(ren)'s current responsibilities.

Session 8: Negotiation and control
* Considering the need to discipline and the kinds of discipline that may or may not be needed in order to maintain a balance of power.
* Focusing upon the consequences of behaviours i.e. children taking responsibility for their actions.
* Use of consequence cards to elicit positive responses.

Session 9: Working in partnership with the school
* Understanding the meaning of working in partnership and clarifying roles, definitions and expectations.

Session 10: Review and personal parenting pacts
  * Identifying and reinforcing positive skills and strategies.
  * Using self-rating questionnaire and the personal parenting pact to set future goals
    and targets.

These ten sessions together provide a 10-week developmental programme in
parenting skills and are appropriate for parents/carers of children of all ages.
The sessions have been designed to be delivered in sequence; however, some can
also be free standing or even combined with other materials or resources you
may have for shorter workshops, depending on the specific needs of the client
group. Where continuity of sessions is required this is indicated in the introduction to the session.

The Structure of the sessions
Each session is generally structured to a 4 to 7 point plan which usually includes
the following: 1. An introduction to the session and, where appropriate, feedback
from the take home activities. 2. An icebreaker. 3. A whole group/smaller group
brainstorming activity. 4. Activity sheets to complete either individually or in
small groups. 5. Follow on thoughts and reflections. 6. Evaluation of session.

Each session comes with detailed notes that provide guidance on how to run the
session, including resource materials required, questions and answers where
appropriate, and handouts that can be photocopied for participants.

The sessions have been designed for groups of between six and fourteen people
who can then be divided into smaller groups of three or four as appropriate.
This information is detailed in each of the session notes. Each session is designed to run for approximately 2 hours.

Resources
For each session the facilitators will need to ensure that the following resources
are available:
  * A quiet room with adequate seating and tables to enable both large group and small
    group work.
  * Flipchart/white board for taking notes or recording ideas.
  * Pens, pencils, masking tape, paper, rubbers, etc.
  * Photocopies of the activities sheets for participants.
  * Folder for each participant to keep worksheets/notes in.
  * Tea, coffee, biscuits as preferred.
  * A session evaluation sheet for each participant (see Appendix).

Facilitators should ensure that they have carefully read the plan for each session in order to gather all the necessary equipment and resources. The above
list details the general requirements for each session but there may be additional resources that need to be prepared.

Success Criteria
It is hoped that the success of the promoting parenting course can be measured
in the following areas:
  * Increasing levels of confidence and self-esteem in parents and their children.
  * Prompting parents to reflect upon their practices, skills and how these may impact

upon children's behaviour, self-esteem and social and emotional development.
* For parents to feel that they can both identify and make use of positive parenting skills and strategies and affect a transfer of these skills from the support group to the home context.
* The existence of a supportive network for parents, which could be sustained or further developed.
* For parents to gain a greater sense of emotional control and awareness.
* For parents to feel more confident in articulating their own needs and strengths and to recognise how they can both positively support others and in turn be supported by them.
* To feel more effective in identifying the signs of potential problems and conflict and in pre-empting and coping more effectively with such situations.
* For parents to be able to discuss their parenting in a more solution focused and insightful way.
* For parents to be able to practise responsible parenting.
* More positive and constructive links with schools.
* For parents to perceive themselves as agents of change, to have begun to effect change and to feel confident in identifying future changes and requirements.
* The development of empathy, cooperation and active listening skills.

Shorter options
If it is not possible or necessary to deliver the 10 sessions in sequence, facilitators might also consider structuring the sessions in 4 units as follows:

Unit 1 (sessions 1-3) "Parents meeting their own needs"
These activities are designed to increase participants' self-awareness, to enable them to reflect on their experiences as parents, examine the models of parenting that they have adopted and the attitudes and beliefs that they have about themselves.

Unit 2 (sessions 4-6) "Our children's needs"
These activities concentrate on participants' understanding of the importance of the emotional relationship between parent and child in developing self-esteem, confidence and independence in their children.

Unit 3 (sessions 7 & 8) "Managing challenging behaviour"
These activities enable participants to examine their beliefs and attitudes in relation to acceptable and unacceptable behaviour, and introduce strategies for encouraging cooperation instead of conflict and defiance and the avoiding of negative labelling and self-attitudes.

Unit 4 (sessions 9 & 10) "Education and the wider community"
Focuses on the parents' role in supporting children's education and social development and considers the essential factors that enable children to have a positive attitude to learning and participation in school. The sessions enable participants to identify their personal learning and development needs and produce appropriate action plans.
Facilitators may wish to run the above described units during the daytime. For example, unit 1 could be presented in three 2 hour sessions over a 1 day period.

Alternatively the unit could be delivered as 3 evening or daytime sessions. These decisions will depend on the needs and requirements of the participants.

However, these suggested structures are merely some of many options and only intended as a guideline. Facilitators may wish to use the materials in other ways, choosing to condense a particular session or to focus particularly on a specific topic.

Moving forward

It is hoped, in line with evaluations of other parenting programmes (Pugh and Smith, 1996) that parents will appreciate both the behavioural aspects of this course and the opportunity to share personal experiences, hopes, difficulties. It is also hoped, that they will have benefited from a focus on developing an emotional vocabulary with which to discuss and evaluate their parenting skills in the context of a safe, non-threatening and non-judgemental group.

However, it is important to emphasise the fact that no one course in parenting skills (including this one) can possibly provide a 'cure-all' for parents who feel that they are not coping with this role particularly well. What the course can offer is a starting point and some practical support in terms of developing more positive self-esteem, belief in one's ability to parent, and the necessary skills and emotional awareness to cope reasonably effectively in a range of situations as a parent.

Perhaps in terms of maintaining and further developing confidence and skills, it will be important for some parents to feel that they have continued access to some form of support or on-going advice. Sutton (1995) identified how the ability to maintain any level of change over time was directly linked to the support on offer.

If parents are to continue to feel further empowered, it will be essential to continue to provide appropriate and adequate levels of on-going support. It may be useful for course facilitator(s) to liaise with both parents and school staff and other professionals in order to ascertain what support is needed for particular groups of parents.. What kind of future support is necessary? What type of support and how and when can this be delivered and by whom? It may well be that parents can and do formulate and maintain their own support network i.e. a weekly or fortnightly group run by parents for parents. However, parents may also wish to engage in other support systems/programmes such as:
* Further work on the development of emotional literacy.
* Further work on developing solution focused thinking and strategies.
* Further workshops which include children.
* Further family workshops and opportunities to learn emotional coaching techniques.
* Further liaison and problem solving sessions with school based staff.

The main aim of any further support will, of course, need to be on the continued development of parents as empowered, confident, skilled and emotionally literate partners in their relationships with their children.

Planning Sessions

The session materials in this pack have been designed as a framework and guide, and are not a cage. It is important that the facilitator negotiates with participants at the first session, the content of the programme so that the group feels that the focus of each session is genuinely up for negotiation. This will enable participants to feel that their individual needs are being addressed, and that the group is actively involved in determining the content of the programme.

The facilitators should familiarise themselves with the materials and ensure that they are clear about the aims and purpose of each activity they plan to use within each session. This will allow the facilitator to be flexible in the way the materials are used and also responsive to the needs of the group in terms of the content and focus of each session. It will also enable participants to be clear about the topics to be covered, which will help to gain and maintain the commitment of group members.

How the programme is planned may well be based on time constraints. The number of weeks or hours available, dependent on participant's time and commitments. The facilitator may also decide that some topics may need to be extended over more than one session to enable the kind of discussion and reflective learning group members require. In this case the facilitator should establish a priority list with the group of the topic areas they would like to cover. If there are no time constraints, the facilitator and group members may wish to extend the programme giving selected topics more than 1 session, (however, it should be noted that the longer programme, the more likelihood of participants dropping out or irregular attendance).

However well sessions are planned, it will be important to respond to the immediate and urgent needs of the groups. It may be that topics need to be re-negotiated or sequenced.

Recruiting to the Group

Often schools and other professionals involved in raising achievement or improving the behaviour of children will identify along with direct support and intervention programmes for the child, a need for providing the parents with strategies to enable them to be confident in their role as parents.

Parenting is a clearly a sensitive and personal issues which most people take for granted. School staff and other professionals involved in the delivery or recruitment of parents/carers to the parenting programme therefore need to be aware of the feelings and needs of their target group. Parents who are anxious about their child's progress or struggling to manage their behaviour may also feel quite vulnerable when entering the school, particularly if staff have expressed concerns about similar difficulties within the school context.

We have found that starting up a supportive group within a school needs extremely sensitive handling. For example it would obviously not be a good idea to approach parents who are feeling angry or excluded and expect them to accept a parenting skills course with open arms and enthusiasm. Neither would it be advisable to run down the list of stage 3 EBD (Emotional Behavioural Difficulties) pupils on the Special Educational Needs register and suggest to their parents that the course would be of great benefit to them.

A more effective way of gaining parents interest and building up a group of parents who will 'buy into' the programme is to involve parents in the initial planning and publicity for the programme. Special Educational Need Coordinators or other staff members who have built up a good relationship with parents may be useful channels for introducing the subject and encouraging parents to participate without appearing to be making judgements about a parent's ability or inability to support their child.

Circulating the information widely within the school as well as sensitive targeting of parents is also effective. Parents are more likely to respond if the aims and content of the programme are made explicit so that parents are clear that by attending they are not labelling themselves as failures or inadequate parents. The publicity information should therefore be positive and not patronising.

When targeting parents from particular culture groups it can be helpful to involve a staff member, or someone from the local community who can speak the language and understand the culture.

From our experience it is important to recognise that establishing a parents' group and gaining credibility with parents takes time.

Newcomers to the group

The facilitators will need to decide, if they are running the full ten week programme, up to what point they will allow new members to join the group. It is generally more difficult and time consuming if new members enter the group after the second or third week, as they will have missed the initial relationship building within the group and the foundation activities required for later sessions. The facilitator will also need to include additional introduction activities so as to assimilate newcomers into the group, which may be tedious for participants who have been attending from the start.

Dealing with unfinished business

Unfinished business refers to any feelings, concerns, anxieties and issues that participants have not being able to air during the session, which may cause discomfort, resentment or misunderstanding. It can be helpful to provide an opportunity for participants to check how group members are feeling, air any concerns about how their contributions have been received by others or how they have understood someone else's input.

The facilitator will need to emphasize that participants should express these from the point of view of how they felt, rather than in an accusing manner. For example, "when you made that remark, I was upset because...", "I found it painful when you talked about...", "I felt you were very supportive when you said ...", "I was really pleased that you felt...", etc.

Session planning

It is useful, regardless of the experience of the facilitator, to have an outline plan for each session as well as overall aims, objectives and success criteria for the whole programme or workshop. It is also important that the learning objectives are clear and that any additional needs of group members are taken into account in the planning. As they get to know the group, the facilitator may find it necessary to select and arrange the activities to suit the preferred learning styles and dynamics of the group members. For example some participants may be more comfortable sharing their ideas in pairs or small groups. In this case the facilitator may wish to carry out some of the whole group activities, such as brainstorming, in small groups, or encourage more paired work.

It is important when deciding to use any method of group work to consider how the activity will be best experienced by the participants. It is also important to ensure that all participants are able to actively engage in learning, so it is vital that the facilitator monitors the contribution of group members and where appropriate asks questions and introduces concerns of individuals.

Group size

The number of participants will affect the dynamics of the group, the time taken to complete activities, and the opportunities to share ideas and views. If the group is too large i.e. over fourteen, it can lose the sense of intimacy that small groups bring, the amount of time that each participant has to share ideas, and how in depth discussions can be. Less than six participants can be problematic, particularly in weeks when one or more group member(s) are unable to attend and when numbers can be uncomfortably low, limiting discussion and effective use of activities.

Cultural and ethnic issues

Some aspects of parenting are closely tied up with cultural, religious and ethnic origin. Participants may therefore have strong feelings about particular ways of bringing up children, and some of the ideas expressed in the activity materials, and by other group members during discussions.

Every effort has been made, where possible, to use examples and materials that reflect a range of ethnic, religious and cultural views and images. The facilitator should encourage participants to appreciate, respect and value the diversity within the group. The facilitator will also need to support group members in focusing on and acknowledging the commonalities that underpin the different approaches to parenting. The facilitator should also be prepared to deal with difficulties which may occur including stereotyping, value-judgements, racism and sexism, which may not be explicit but should nevertheless be challenged and included in the group rules.

Feedback and evaluation of sessions

All participants should be encouraged to complete the evaluation sheet at the end of each session (see Appendix). Alternatively, it may be more appropriate to ask the group to complete the feedback collectively or at the end of each block of sessions.

If there are any negative comments, facilitators will have to carefully consider how to approach these and will certainly need to reflect upon their approach/ delivery and possibly adapt as appropriate.

It will be important to address any concerns at the start of the next session so that participants feel that their views are being listened to and understood.

If a particularly sensitive issue is raised by one parent (and they may have made it clear that they wish to discuss the matter further), the course participants may wish to allocate some additional time for this purpose e.g. a one to one chat/ discussion in order to address concerns.

Handling difficult moments

At times there may be difficult or tense moments when group members may appear despondent or emotional. Silence in a group can be perceived as awkward and uncomfortable. Many people tend to want to fill silence with either laughter or superficial chatter. However, silence can be very useful as it allows participants time to think deeply about an issue or situation before responding. It can also show respect and acknowledgement for something said which is significant and pertinent. Facilitators should ensure that the group is aware of the usefulness of silence as this will help participants to feel less uncomfortable or threatened by it.

The facilitator should explain to the group that expressing strong emotions such as crying and getting angry, etc is acceptable and at times necessary and that the group should be a safe place for all group members to express themselves. It is particularly important that the facilitator has considered how to handle these situations positively and can be an example for the group, who will, through the programme, be developing these skills.

Roles in the group

In most groups people make conscious or more often unconscious decisions about the roles they take on within the group. It is important that the facilitator is aware of the different roles found in groups and makes participants aware of the roles they are adopting consciously or unconsciously or in some cases being given by other members of the group. Participants may take on some or all of the following roles:

listener	pacifier	clarifier	gossip	stimulator
optimist	questioner	helper	timekeeper	delayer
challenger	risk taker	anecdote	mother	father
time hugger	child	intimidator	leader	scapegoat
client/patient	underminer	catalyst	silent member	informer
nurturer	know all	pessimist	mediator	joker

The roles that participants take in the group (and these can change) can be positive or damaging to the group dynamics. It may be helpful in the early stages of the programme to discuss group roles and dynamics within the group and encourage participants to identify the roles they take on and how they feel about them. The facilitator will need to explain to the group that this is an important part of the programme. Participants need to be aware of the way they are behaving particularly if they are taking on roles that are counter productive, insensitive or damaging to the group or individual members.

Group dynamics

The group dynamics, i.e. the way individuals behave as a group, are often subtle and complex. The facilitator should observe both the verbal exchanges within the group and the non-verbal cues such as the body language of group members as this can provide useful information about how participants are feeling. It can also help the facilitator gauge whether the session activities and pace are engaging for the group members or if participants are struggling with the content or process.

Setting up childcare/crèche

It is worth considering the possibilities of providing childcare for the group sessions. For many parents/carers this facility may be the deciding factor as to whether they can commit themselves to the full programme or attend at all.

Setting up a crèche/childcare does require resources and planning so may not be an option for all groups. It may be advisable to first consider what provision is already available that the group could utilize such as an established crèche, play group or nursery. This will obviously depend on the location of the group and resources available. If childcare needs to be set up specifically for the group, it is important that the group or programme organizer seek advice from the appropriate local services on regulations concerning adult/child ratios and Health and Safety. Arrangements will also need to be made for introduction and settling of children into the crèche before the start of the sessions.

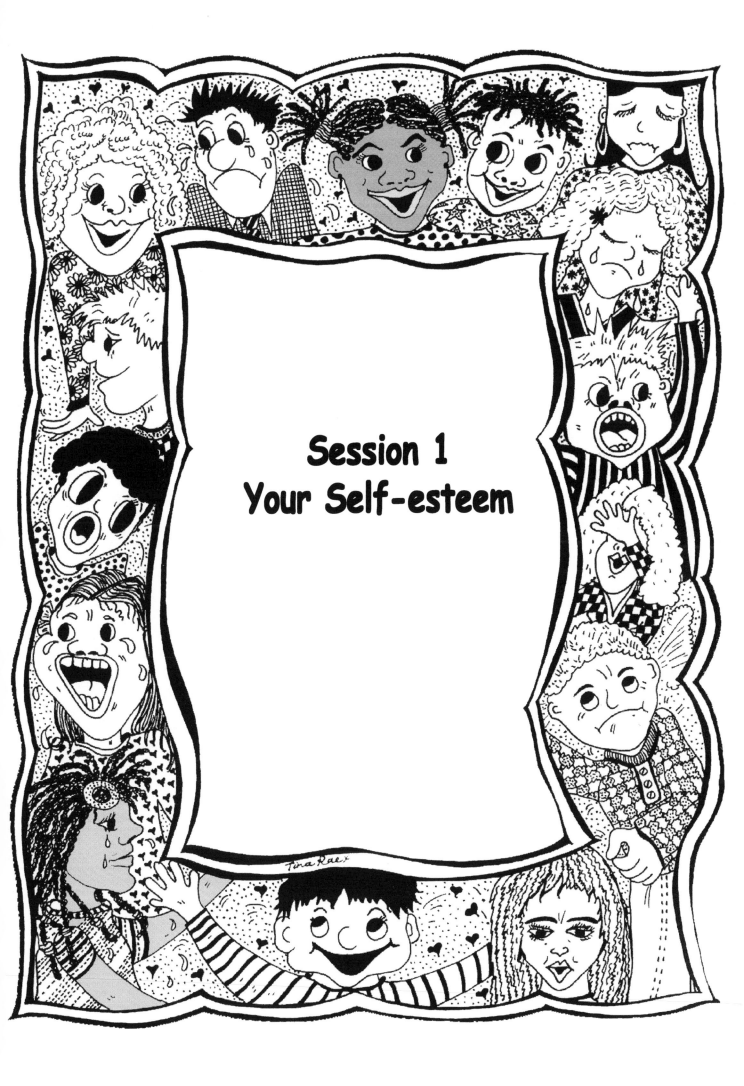

Session 1
Your Self-esteem

Tina Rae

Session 1: Your self-esteem

Group session: 2 hours This session is divided into 6 sections as follows:
1. Introduction.
2. Icebreaker.
3. Identifying and setting group rules.
4. Brainstorming activity: What is good self-esteem?
5. Quick quiz.
6. Follow on thought: The scaling activity.

1. Introduction

This initial session is extremely important in terms of setting the climate for the programme as a whole. Whether or not the facilitator chooses to run all or part of the programme in or out of sequence, it is vital that this first session highlights the positive and constructive nature of the course and the way in which all participants' views, ideas and contributions will be both valued and respected. When setting "group rules" with participants, the facilitator will need to highlight the relevant course content and the importance that will be placed upon protecting, reinforcing and developing the self-esteem of all participants. The session allows for the clarification of the term "self-esteem" and encourages participants to explore their own confidence and current levels of self-esteem alongside reflecting upon their own childhood relationships with parents and carers and how these "models" may have affected their own parenting styles and skills.

2. Icebreaker

At the start of the sessions it is important to breakdown barriers as quickly as possible and to create an atmosphere where participants feel relaxed and at ease. This is particularly important on parenting skills programmes where a supportive and trusting relationship needs to be developed between participants so that they can openly discuss issues, share experiences and information about themselves and their families.

The purpose of the icebreaker activity is to get participants talking to each other and sharing information about themselves. The activity can be used at the start of any parenting programme as it is intended to start the group thinking about their needs as parents, and to begin practising active listening which is an important part of the learning process that enables everyone to contribute to the session. It is also intended to reassure participants that they will be in a safe and ethical environment and to introduce the importance of confidentiality within the group which will be further discussed in the session when establishing the group rules.

For this activity the group facilitator presents a set of questions for the participants to discuss and answer. The questions should be open ended to allow participants to express any fears, hopes, concerns or expectations that they might have and to identify their own learning goals. Questions may include the following:
* What do I hope to get out of the sessions?
* What are my fears or concerns about the programme/sessions?
* What are my expectations about the programme/sessions?

* What will enable me to achieve my learning goals?
* What will hinder me in contributing to the sessions?
* What do I want from other people in the group?

The facilitator in introducing the activity can explain to the group that their responses will be helpful in ensuring that the individual and collective needs of group members are addressed through the programme.

The facilitator should provide participants with a question sheet and ask them to write down their responses. At the same time the facilitators should also note down their own answers to share with the group.

The group can then be divided into pairs or small groups (ideally with partners that they do not know). Each group is then asked to discuss their responses and note them down on flipchart paper. It should be explained that they do not have to reach a consensus and there will be differences as well as similarities. Each group is then asked to present the points they have listed. Typical responses may include:
    * Not feeling confident speaking in groups.
    * Other people thinking they are boring or not very clever.
    * Disclosing personal things about themselves.
    * Not understanding.
    * Not getting on with other people in the group.
    * Being asked to write on the flip chart.
    * Wanting to become a more confident parent.
    * Being able to deal more effectively with my child's behaviour.
    * Meeting other parents who are in a similar situation.
    * Making new friends and getting support.
    * Gain more confidence.
    * Sharing concerns and developing practical strategies.

The facilitator guides the group through each of the points raised and invites other group members to comment and asks for clarification or elaboration on points where necessary. It is important for the facilitator to acknowledge and address issues that arise, as part of the process of identifying the needs and aspirations of group members and developing appropriate group rules.

If the group does not raise the issue of confidentiality the facilitator may find it helpful to introduce the concept as a lead into the group rules brainstorming activity.

3. Identifying and setting group rules
It is vital that everyone involved in the programme has an opportunity at the very start to identify and agree a set of group rules. Course facilitators can initially clarify the main aims of the programme, the basic structure and format of the sessions. It should also be explained to participants that the programme is designed to offer a supportive framework in which they can gain confidence in their own skills, further develop useful strategies and became more aware as to how they can make a real difference to the emotional well-being of their children. This message is reinforced in Daniel Goleman's book 'Emotional Intelligence' (1996) -all parents can make significant differences to their children's emotional health and the way in which they develop positive relationships with

both peers and adults.

In outlining the programme in this way course facilitators should stress the fact that they are not to be regarded as 'experts' who will 'sit and tell' but rather as working in partnership with the group to develop the skills, self-esteem and confidence of all participants. The need to establish a series of agreed group rules in order to promote and protect the self-esteem of each individual should be emphasised at the beginning of the programme/session.

Participants and course facilitators can 'brainstorm' and record a series of group rules that may include some of the following ideas:
* Everyone needs to encourage each other to have a say.
* We all need to listen and respect each other's point of view -even if those views are very different to our own.
* We need to agree to challenge any stereotyping in a constructive way.
* We need to treat each other's ideas, suggestions and examples with respect and in confidence so that we all feel secure in talking about our experiences and ourselves.
* Everyone needs to help each other to find real solutions.
* We need to promote everyone's self-esteem and confidence.
* We should not be frightened to disagree.
* We need to co-operate and work together, sharing ideas and recognising that we ALL have something to offer.
* We agree that we are all of value and all have the right to be ourselves and to be accepted.
Copies of the agreed rules should be given to all participants (session 2).

4. Brainstorming activity: What is good self-esteem? (Worksheet 1)
The aim here is to elicit participants' views. Course facilitators can record ideas and responses on a flip chart or participants can use the brainstorming sheet provided to record their responses either individually or as a member of a pair/smaller group. If the latter option is chosen, it will be necessary to ask the smaller group to feedback once ideas have been discussed and recorded. It will be interesting to note any similarities, differences, agreements and disagreements as to what participants think 'good self-esteem' is. Contributions might include some of the following:
* Feeling good about yourself.
* Liking yourself: feeling loved/valued.
* Thinking others like you.
* Thinking that you look good.
* Feeling that you have good relationships with other adults and your child(ren).
* You feel confident about talking about new things.
* You generally enjoy life.
* Feeling happy.
* Not worrying about what others think of you.
* Not putting yourself down.
* Feeling positive about life.
* Not feeling down/jealous of other's lives, etc.

5. Quick quiz. (Worksheet 2)
Although this quiz is presented as a 'fun' activity in the style of a magazine quiz (it is adapted from Jenny Mosely & Eileen Gillibrand's book 'She Who Dares

Wins' [Thorsons 1995]), it does allow for quite a serious session of reflection and evaluation. Participants can, as a result, identify exactly where they consider themselves to be in terms of confidence, self-esteem, relationships, coping strategies and general level of well-being.

The quiz requires participants to rate themselves on the following:
* People liking you/having good relationships.
* Ability to cope with new situations.
* Coping with criticism and jealousy.
* Putting yourself down (and others!).
* Feeling happy, hopeless and miserable.
* Attempting to impress and please others.
* Feeling that you have missed out and have not had the same chances/opportunities as others.

Some participants may identify themselves, as being especially vulnerable in some of these areas and course facilitators will need to be particularly sensitive in ensuring that appropriate additional support is made available to these participants. Clearly, this would be determined in consultation with the group member in a private context after the session. Alongside highlighting any areas that participants might like to change and develop, this activity also logically leads on to the final follow on thoughts sheet which can either be completed at the end of the session/can be given to participants to complete at home.

6. Follow-on thoughts: The scaling activity. (Worksheet 3)
Participants are required to rate themselves on a scale of 0-10, 0 would indicate that they feel totally negative about how they are coping as a parent, 5 would indicate that they generally feel okay but recognize the need to make improvements, 10 would imply perfection!

This rating system needs to be clearly explained to participants prior to starting the activity. Once they have recorded a rating they are then able to proceed in identifying the following:
* What they have done so far in order to get to where they are.
* Where they would like to be.
* How they can get there i.e. what do their own personal targets need to be.

Example: Sandra aged 42
* I am on 4.
* This is because I know I shout a lot at my kids, especially in the evenings when I came in from work and I am knackered. I don't seem to have the patience to listen to them and even when I do help them with homework I can feel I am getting irritated when they don't get it.
* I would like to be on 7. I can get there if I try to reach these targets.
* Ask my mum if she'd pick the kids up from school one night each week so I can have some time to relax and then make them a nice dinner when they get in.
* Try to think how they are feeling a bit more and tell them how I feel instead of shouting it.
* Try to set aside 30 minutes each night when I sit down with them and listen to them without thinking I have got to be telling them stuff.

The final part of the follow-on thoughts sheet asks participants to reflect upon their own childhood and their relationship with parents/carers in order to evaluate the extent to which they may have based their own parenting skills on these models. This thinking activity is designed to initiate careful reflection in preparation for the initial brainstorming activity of session 2 -What made me?

Brainstorm
Our group rules are...

*

_____

*

_____

*

_____

*

_____

*

_____

*

_____

*

_____

Session 1: Worksheet 1   Brainstorm activity

Think and discuss!
How do you know if someone has good self-esteem?

How do they feel, act, think and communicate?

What is good self-esteem?

Session 1: Worksheet 2　　　Your self-esteem - Quick Quiz

Please answer the following questions. Think carefully!
    Tick box A = Never
    Tick box B = Sometimes
    Tick box C = Often
    Tick box D = Always

1. Do you think that other people like you ?
    A ☐   B ☐   C ☐   D ☐

2. Do you think that you have 'good' relationships at home?
    A ☐   B ☐   C ☐   D ☐

3. Do you feel that you have 'good' friends?
    A ☐   B ☐   C ☐   D ☐

4. If asked to try/do something new, do you feel confident?
    A ☐   B ☐   C ☐   D ☐

5. Do you consider yourself to be a capable sort of person?
    A ☐   B ☐   C ☐   D ☐

6. Can you admit to making mistakes?
    A ☐   B ☐   C ☐   D ☐

7. Do you trust most people?
    A ☐   B ☐   C ☐   D ☐

8. Are you happy about meeting new people/developing new friendships?
    A ☐   B ☐   C ☐   D ☐

9. Do you generally feel happy in your life?
    A ☐   B ☐   C ☐   D ☐

10. Are you able to relax and enjoy yourself?
    A ☐   B ☐   C ☐   D ☐

Now add up your score   A = 1 point
    B = 2 points
    C = 3 points
    D = 4 points

Total = _____

Section 2

Tick box A = Never   B = Sometimes   C = Often D = Always

11. Do you feel jealous of other people and their lives?

A ☐   B ☐   C ☐   D ☐

12. Do you feel miserable if other people criticise you?

A ☐   B ☐   C ☐   D ☐

13. Do you feel that you 'miss out' on the chances that other people got?

A ☐   B ☐   C ☐   D ☐

14. Are you worried about what other people think about you?

A ☐   B ☐   C ☐   D ☐

15. When in a group situation, do you find yourself feeling excluded?

A ☐   B ☐   C ☐   D ☐

16. Do you feel that your life is hopeless?

A ☐   B ☐   C ☐   D ☐

17. Do you think that you need to impress other people?

A ☐   B ☐   C ☐   D ☐

18. Do you feel 'fed up' at the end of each day?

A ☐   B ☐   C ☐   D ☐

19. Do you feel that other people just don't understand you?

A ☐   B ☐   C ☐   D ☐

20. Do you feel that other people have better relationships than you do?

A ☐   B ☐   C ☐   D ☐

21. Do you dislike other people (without telling anyone about it?)

A ☐   B ☐   C ☐   D ☐

22. Do you feel depressed about your life situation?

A ☐   B ☐   C ☐   D ☐

23. Do you feel shy/awkward in some situations?

A ☐   B ☐   C ☐   D ☐

24. Do you make excuses for not doing things you know you would like to do?

A ☐   B ☐   C ☐   D ☐

25. Do you tend to keep your problems a secret?

A ☐   B ☐   C ☐   D ☐

26. Do you think that you have to impress others with the way that you behave?

A ☐   B ☐   C ☐   D ☐

27. Do you try to please other people all the time?

A ☐   B ☐   C ☐   D ☐

28. Do you 'put yourself down' to other people?

A ☐   B ☐   C ☐   D ☐

Now add up your score   A = 4 points B = 3 points C = 2 points D = 1 point

Total = _____   **Overall Total** _____

RESULTS! SCORE YOURSELF!

Score 28-45

You have low self-esteem so now you really do need to begin to work on it in order to become a happier and more confident person. START TO THINK POSITIVE. You can change and begin to feel good about yourself and your life in general. You can start by making very small changes in order to build a better you and to change the way you feel, not just about yourself but also how you think others feel about you. Identify 3 areas and set yourself realistic goals. Time to go for it!

Score 46-75

Your self-esteem is a bit up and down. You need to start to feel more in control of your life and more confident about your coping strategies. It's now time to build yourself up and put yourself forward more. Those things which have made you feel a bit fragile now need to be recognised, articulated and swept away. It's time to clean up and shape up. Identify those fragile spots and formulate an action plan which details small and manageable steps on the path to personal change and growth. Go for it!

Score 76-96

Your self-esteem is okay but you probably still lack confidence in a few key areas. These now need to be identified and sorted out so that you can become more confident and feel happier about who you are. Then you will be in a position to really make the most of all those opportunities. Time to build yourself up just that bit higher. Go for it!

Score 97-112

Your self-esteem is fine! Marvellous! You are generally a positive person and you feel confident about yourself and your life. Consider setting yourself some new goals, make them bigger and better. Go for it!

**Session 1. Worksheet 3 Follow-on thoughts:
The scaling activity Think and reflect.**

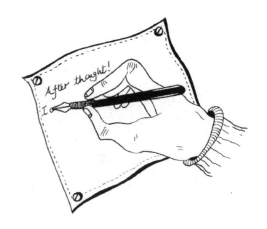

Rate yourself! How do you currently
think you are coping as a parent?

1	2	3	4	5	6	7	8	9	10

Questions to answer

1. Where am I now?

2. What have I done in order to get to that point?
   I have ...

3. Where would I like to be?

4. How can I get there?
   How do I need to change:
   My targets to reach that point are: ...

   a.

   b.

   c.

   d.

   e.

Pause and reflect.
Think about your own childhood and your relationships with your parents/carers. Have you based your own parenting skills and relationships on these models? Has anyone/anything else particularly influenced you?

Session 2
Your models
and influences

Session 2 Your models and influences

Group session: 2 hours This session is divided into 6 sections as follows:
1. Introduction.
2. Ice breaker.
3. Brainstorming activity: Identifying What has made me?
4. Major Models.
5. The parent job description.
6. Follow on thought: What is a positive parent'?

The activities in this session follow on from session 1 but are also suitable for shorter programmes or workshops and can be used as part of an introductory or taster session.

1. Introduction
At the start of this session, the facilitators should provide each participant with a copy of the group rules agreed in session 1. These should be reinforced and participants should be given the opportunity to make any further contributions or amendments to the list. A week's reflection on the initial session may well have prompted further thoughts and ideas.

The facilitators may then wish to introduce the importance of the parenting role, perhaps covering some of the points raised in the following two paragraphs. Being a parent is one of the most important jobs that a person will ever do. The responsibility of being a parent is enormous and is taken on without any formal training. Although the concept of parenting has been used for centuries and is regarded as a natural process within most societies, how individuals acquire the knowledge, skills and qualities needed for this role is, in most cases, a matter of chance.

People gain their experience through trial and error and continue to learn as they go along. It is important for parents/carers to appreciate how well they are doing and to be reassured that there are no 'right' ways of parenting that can be prescribed and that there will always be ups and downs which is all part of family life.

This session aims to explore the concept of parenting, identifying what the role entails, how participants acquire their parenting skills, and the beliefs and values they adopt from experiences and relationships with family and other significant people. The activities are intended to get participants to consider the impact of their experience of being parented on the attitudes, values and beliefs they hold about 'good parenting'.

2. Icebreaker
This activity is useful for helping participants understand the links between childhood experiences and the beliefs, attitudes and expectations they currently hold.

Participants are encouraged to think about the role of myths and stories and sayings from their childhood that have had significance, impact or influence on them as adults.

The facilitator should emphasise that this is a lighthearted activity intended to encourage participants to think about influences that shape our views, values and beliefs.

In pairs, participants are asked to note down myths, sayings and stories that they enjoyed, found uncomfortable or memorable. The groups should then compare their lists and discuss how they recall receiving the myth, saying or story and what had been the effect at the time. Contributions that we have received in the past include:
* Women must get married and have children.
* Pride comes before a fall.
* Unfeminine or powerful women must be gay.
* Hard work never killed anybody.
* The myth of the tortoise and the hare.
* Spare the rod and spoil the child.
* Myth about beauty which perpetuates the view of white, blonde, slim women as being beautiful, e.g. Snow White, Goldilocks, etc.
* The Seven Dwarfs -presenting negative representations of disability.
* Stories of women being dependent upon men for security and protection e.g. Rapunzel, Sleeping Beauty.
* Her crowning glory -the notion that women have to have beautiful hair.
* Children should be seen not heard.

The facilitator can point out that myths, sayings and stories contain social norms, values of their time and society from which they originate. It can also be explained that our perceptions of events, people and achievements are informed by our experiences, culture, language, family and social status.

The response may include some of the following:
* Messages about gender roles.
* Views about different kinds of people in society.
* Messages about disabilities e.g. dwarfs, hunch back of Notredame, etc.
* Stereotypes of beauty.
* Moral values of 'good' and 'bad'.
* Racial and cultural biases.

3.Brainstorming activity:Identifying what has made me? (Worksheet 1)
The way people think and talk about themselves can affect their sense of well-being and confidence in their ability to deal with the challenges presented to them in the parenting role.

This activity enables group members to first identify individually the main models and influences that have had a significant impact on their self-image, attitudes, beliefs and values. Participants will be able to assess how powerful these influences are and consider the similarities and differences in experiences within the group.

The facilitator should introduce the activity by explaining to the group that the purpose of the activity is to develop an understanding of how our experiences and memories of our childhood relationships and other events in our lives can have a significant impact on our perception of ourselves as an individual and as a parent.

The facilitator should also emphasise that group members have control over the breadth and depth of disclosure and do not have to talk about uncomfortable experiences (participants should be referred back to the group rules, in particular the one regarding confidentiality). It will be important to point out that some reflection on their own experience is necessary to enable them to develop their self-awareness.

Participants are then asked to spend ten minutes individually reflecting on main influences and role models that they feel contributed in making them the people they are.

The participants are then divided into groups of three or four and asked to spend fifteen minutes describing to each other their personal experiences, noting down the similarities and differences in experiences and key points for discussion with the whole group.

The facilitator should then bring the participants back together as a whole group and discuss the points identified in the subgroups, recording on the flip-chart the key points identified and any other issues that arise.

Participants should then be asked to discuss reasons for the similarities and differences. It is likely that their responses will introduce issues concerning the influence of; culture, religion, race, gender and other social influences such as the media, government intervention and education.

The group should then brainstorm the ways in which models and influences can significantly affect people's self image and confidence as parents. The ideas should be listed on the flipchart with participants circling those that they feel are the most important.

4. Major models. (Worksheet 2)
This activity builds on the activity 'What's made me?' in developing participants' understanding and awareness of the significant events in their lives that have helped determine their self-image, perceptions and attitudes. The activity also enables the participants to analyse in more depth how this is reflected in their current style of parenting.

It is helpful when introducing this kind of activity for the facilitator to provide an example from their own experience to help the group feel more comfortable about self-disclosure.

To start the group thinking more in depth about the impact of events, relationships and other social factors on their current behaviour as a parent, participants should be given 5-10 minutes to complete the Major Models activity sheet individually. This requires them to consider the role of their parents, teachers, friends and other social influences in shaping their attitudes, beliefs and values.

When they have completed the exercise divide the group into twos and ask each pair to discuss the responses they have listed in each square for 10 minutes. Bring the participants back together and discuss the responses from each pair focusing on how the influences identified by participants are reflected in their behaviour. The facilitator should encourage the group to think about why particular people, events or information have had positive or negative influence. From this discussion, participants will recognise common factors that characterise relationships and situations as either positive or negative and how these affect our perceptions and subjective being.

At the end of the activity the facilitator should make clear to the group that the purpose of the activity was to increase awareness of themselves and understanding of the process by which attitudes are formed and how these in turn influence our behaviour and is not intended as an opportunity to apportion blame or create resentment within individuals.

5. The parent job description

For this activity the facilitator divides the participants into groups of 3's or 4's. The groups are given 10 to 15 minutes to discuss and list on flipchart paper the roles and responsibilities of a parent. It is important that the facilitator makes clear that they do not have to reach a consensus, and whilst there may be many similarities in opinions there will probably be some differences.

When the group have completed the list, the facilitator then asks them to display their flipchart so the whole group can see their responses. Allow the group to discuss each of the listed points and to include any additional views that arise. Participants are likely to list a wide range of roles, responsibilities and activities carried out by parents. The facilitator may need to remind the group of roles or activities that were not included and are taken for granted, for example: coordinating schedules, providing emotional stability, etc. (if these are not already identified).

The following list is typical of the answers you can expect although it is not exhaustive:

provider	cook	friend	educator	gardener	housekeeper
nurse	taxi	cleaner	counsellor	advisor	childminder.

The facilitator should ask the group to keep this as a reminder for future activities and reference as the list represents the complex and demanding role that they fulfil as parents. The facilitator should also stress that parenting embraces many of the skills used by a number of professionals and requires many of the same qualities and skills required for effective communication.

6. Follow on thoughts: What is a positive parent? (Worksheet 3)

This activity encourages participants to focus on their individual needs as they consider the qualities they associate with being a positive and effective parent. This activity can either be carried out as part of the session or as a reflection activity in the participant's own time. The facilitator should advise the group that they should note down their immediate responses as honestly as possible so that these can be used as a source of reference and measurement of their development throughout the sessions.

Session 2. Worksheet 1 Brainstorming Activity

What's made me?

What are my main models and influences?

Think, discuss and record.

Think and discuss
   * Which of these do you feel are most significant and why?
   * Share your ideas in the group and consider if and why there are any similarities and differences in your experiences.

Session 2. Worksheet 2 Major Models

Consider these 4 significant influences on your current parenting style. Identify the individuals concerned and how their behaviour may have impacted upon you. Finally, identify how you think these influences can be seen in your own behaviour as a parent.

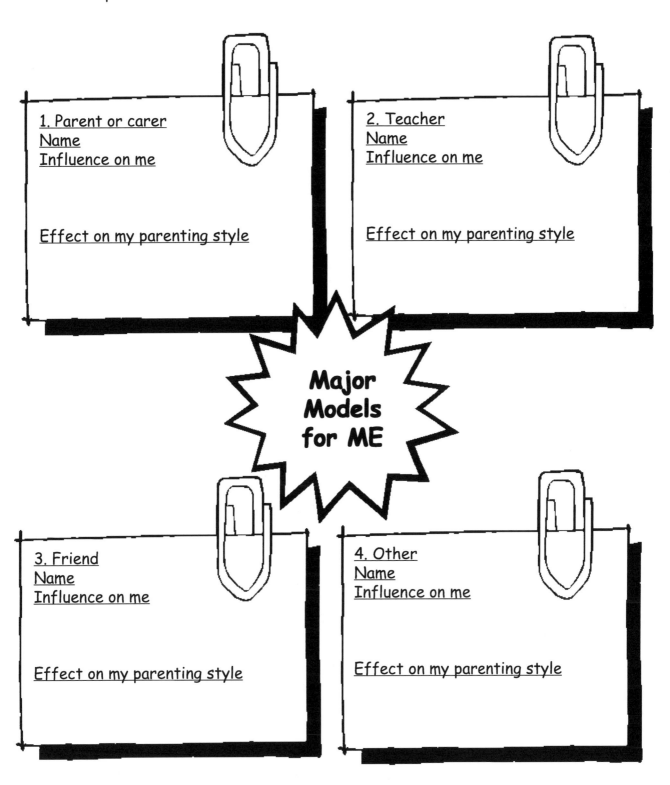

1. Parent or carer
Name
Influence on me

Effect on my parenting style

2. Teacher
Name
Influence on me

Effect on my parenting style

Major
Models
for ME

3. Friend
Name
Influence on me

Effect on my parenting style

4. Other
Name
Influence on me

Effect on my parenting style

* Are these influences positive/negative and why?
* Discuss and share experiences and ideas in the group.

Complete a personal brainstorm.
What do you think a 'positive parent' is?
What makes someone a 'good parent'?
List the qualities that you feel are most vital.

Pause and reflect

Be Positive! Constructive!
Which of these qualities do you think you have
    a) Some of the time
    b) All of the time
    c) Rarely

Identify 3 areas you would like to work on or feel more positive about.
Identify the resources and support you will need to make these changes.

Number 1.	Number 2.	Number 3.
Resources/support	Resources/support	Resources/support

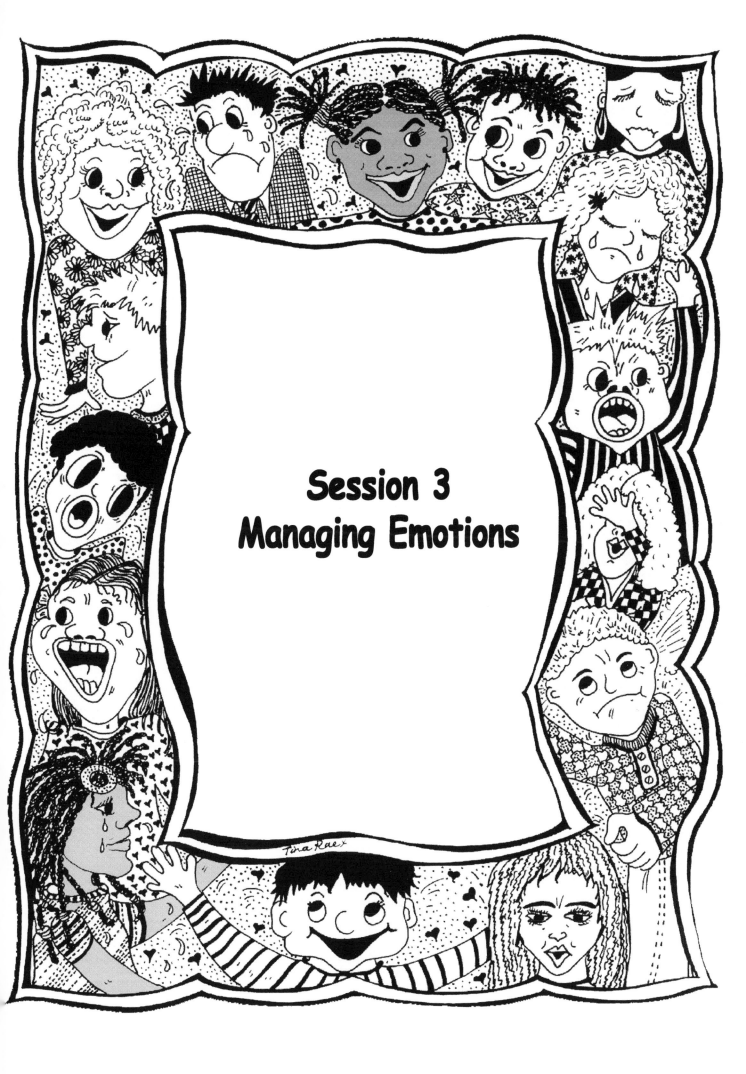

Session 3
Managing Emotions

Tina Rae

Session 3: Managing Emotions

Group session: 2 hours. This session is divided into 5 sections as follows:
1. Introduction.
2. Icebreaker.
3. Brainstorming activity: Emotional triggers.
4. Self Reflection activity.
5. Follow on thought: Focus on conflict - Communicating feelings.

1. Introduction

This session focuses on the importance of developing emotional literacy, which is an important and useful skill that enables parents to effectively and more confidently deal with relationships and manage their children's behaviour. Being emotionally literate means that a person is aware of their own feelings and those of others and that they can modify their responses and behaviour in order to function appropriately in a given social context.

Being self-reflective and being aware of what triggers certain feelings and emotions in oneself is focused upon in this session.

Participants are given the opportunity to identify personal emotional triggers and to consider strategies for coping more effectively with conflict and strong feelings. Most importantly participants are encouraged to identify how they can further engender positive feelings and behaviour in their children.

2. Ice breaker

This activity is intended to focus group members on how they are feeling at the start of the session and to help participants understand the impact of positive feedback in creating a sense of well-being and positive self-esteem.

The facilitator should place large sheets of flip chart paper with several large empty speech bubbles drawn on them around the room. After this participants are asked to write down how they are feeling, (alternatively they may wish to draw a symbol which represents their feelings.) When each of the group members has completed the task, the facilitator should then supply each participant with a sheet of A4 paper and ask them to write their name at the top of the page and to then stick the sheet onto their backs. The participants are then asked to write a positive statement about each group member on the sheets pinned onto their backs. The facilitator should explain that the statements must not be seen or discussed with the person it is written about at this stage and group members will not be asked to identify their written statements.

When all participants have completed the task, the facilitator should then bring the group back together and discuss the feelings group members have expressed in the speech bubbles. At this point participants may or may not wish to identify themselves with their written statements. A range of feelings will have been expressed. The facilitator may wish to make it clear to the group that the activity is not intended as any form of psychological analysis of group members and that to gain awareness of one's feelings and feeling states is the important aim of the activity.

When all the responses have been discussed, the group should then be asked to remove the A4 sheets pinned on participants' backs and to consider the list of positive statements written about each of them.

The facilitator can then ask group members to compare their feeling's statements with those compiled about them by the rest of the group. Participants will generally feel more valued when reading through the statements and they may also be surprised by the attributes assigned to them in the positive list of statements.

The facilitator can conclude the activity by explaining that positive feelings can be a source of energy and motivation and can provide the confidence needed for making decisions. Negative feelings can become knots inside us blocking rational decision-making.

3. Brainstorming activity: Emotional triggers. (Worksheet 1)

For this activity the facilitator should distribute worksheet 1 and ask participants to find a partner to work with, ideally someone with whom they have not worked previously and then ask them to think of a real-life situation, events and people who have caused them to experience the following feelings: happiness, excitement, surprise, love, joy, fear, anger, stress, jealously, and rejection. Participants should then be asked to discuss their responses listed on the worksheet with the whole group. The facilitator may need to prompt participants to ensure that they focus equally on both the uncomfortable and the comfortable emotions.

When the activity has been completed the responses should be collected and recorded on the flipchart. The facilitator should ask the participants to think about why certain situations and people trigger particular kinds of emotions. Responses may include:
   * Unhappy memories.
   * Similarities between people.
   * Messages and labels given to individuals.
   * Attitudes, beliefs and values.

The facilitator should then explain that communication involves thinking, feeling, speaking and listening. We communicate through a combination of verbal and non-verbal cues, which we consciously and subconsciously send and receive. The facilitator can also point out to the group that talking about emotions is sometimes difficult for some people, not just because the emotions are painful or unpleasant but often because we do not often verbally express feelings and sometimes we may have difficulty finding words to express ourselves.

4. Self Reflection Activity. (Worksheet 2)

This worksheet is designed for participants to complete individually. It gives participants the opportunity to reflect on how their behaviour, actions and emotional states can influence how their children feel and behave. In considering the impact of their emotions on themselves and others, participants are prompted to appreciate the important link between feelings, emotions and the behaviour of their children.

The following parent's survival tips may be a positive means of drawing together the links that parents have made:
* Taking time out for yourself.
* Reminding yourself of events and conversations that feel good.
* Remembering that there's no such thing as a perfect parent.
* We all get it wrong sometimes.
* When things go wrong it provides us with learning opportunities.
* Your best is all you can do.
* You have rights too.
* If you are happy in what you are doing, you are more able to make someone else happy.
* It's okay to say no.
* You can ask for help.

5. Follow on thoughts: Focus on conflict - Communicating feelings. (Worksheet 3)

This take home activity focuses on raising participant's awareness of how they manage conflict situations and how they might cope more effectively with the unpleasant or negative feelings these situations can create. The facilitator in introducing the activity may wish to re-emphasise the powerful influence that our beliefs, values and attitudes have in creating and shaping our perceptions of the world and in influencing our responses to events, situations and people.

The notion of positive and negative perceptions can be introduced. The facilitator may want to begin by discussing how one's perception of events and situations can be optimistic, expansive and outward looking so that experiences are viewed as positive learning opportunities. Alternatively, our perceptions can be pessimistic, narrow or inward and can limit our ability to think imaginatively and confidently when it comes to working through solutions and dealing with conflict.

For example, one parent indicated that she felt that her child's literacy difficulties were a reflection of her own lack of skills in this area and that she regarded the support offered by the school as both patronising and intrusive. This contrasted to another parent's view of her child's needs. This parent was delighted that school staff had identified these needs so promptly and was keen to learn and develop her own strategies and skills in order to support her child at home. Her perception of the situation was positive and she felt empowered by the support offered by the Special Educational Needs Coordinator and her child's class teacher.

Participants should be made aware that the purpose of the activity is to focus on strategies for developing positive perceptions and responses to conflict and stressful situations they may experience as parents.

The facilitator should explain to the group that the intention is not to force change, but to encourage group members to explore possibilities and options. It is important to be conscious of the feelings of group members and to ensure that in exploring areas of themselves, participants are not inadvertently made to feel vulnerable and left without a safety net.

Each participant is provided with worksheet 3 and asked to individually brainstorm when they tend to respond in a negative way to conflict with their children and other adults and how they could manage the situations and the feelings these situations arouse more effectively.

The facilitator then asks participants to share their responses and explore the role emotions play in their own performance as parents at the start of next session. Participants can then consider the strategies suggested for developing emotional awareness and managing conflict (by themselves or with other members of the group) that they might use with their child(ren) in the future.

Participants may wish to identify some personal goals, will involve making use of their emotional awareness skills more effectively as parents and as individuals.

Session 3. Worksheet 1 Brainstorming Activity Emotional Triggers!

Identify situations/events/people who have caused you to experience the following feelings:

POSITIVE	NEGATIVE

Happiness
   * Who/What?
   * When?
   * Why?
	Fear
	   * Who/What?
	   * When?
	   * Why?

Excitement
   * Who/What?
   * When?
   * Why?
	Anger
	   * Who/What?
	   * When?
	   * Why?

Surprise
   * Who/What?
   * When?
   * Why?
	Stress
	   * Who/What?
	   * When?
	   * Why?

Love
   * Who/What?
   * When?
   * Why?
	Jealousy
	   * Who/What?
	   * When?
	   * Why?

Joy
   * Who/What?
   * When?
   * Why?
	Rejection
	   * Who/What?
	   * When?
	   * Why?

Session 3. Worksheet 2 Self-reflect

How do I make others feel?
Consider how your behaviours, actions and emotional states
impact upon your child/children.
Complete the following chart:

My child/children felt	When?	What did you do?	Why?
Happy			
Excited			
Loved			
Valued			
Scared			
Angry			
Jealous			
Rejected			

Think of 3 things that you can do in order to ensure that your child/children can experience feeling loved and valued on a daily basis. Share your ideas in the group. Consider if and why there are any similarities and differences in your ideas. Record your ideas on the reverse of this sheet.

Session 3. Worksheet 3 Focus on Conflict - Communicating Feelings

Brainstorm.

When do you tend to respond in a negative way to conflicts with your child/children and other adults?

How can you cope more effectively with such feelings?

Complete the following statements:

1. I get angry/upset with my children when:

2. I get angry/upset with other adults when they:

3. They/he/she know(s) I am angry because:

4. I could help myself more if/by:

5. I could help my child/children more if/by:

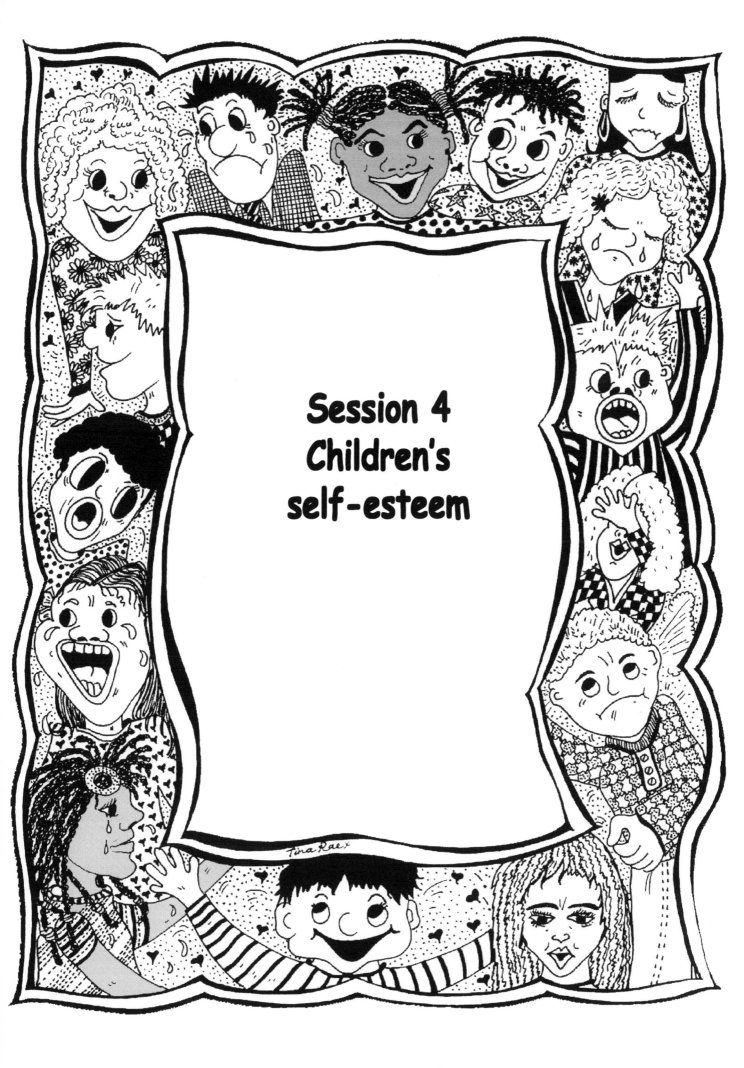

Session 4
Children's
self-esteem

Tina Rae x

Session 4:   Children's self-esteem

Group session: 2 hours This session is divided into 6 sections as follows:

1. Discussion of Worksheet 3 from Session 3.
2. Introduction.
3. Icebreaker.
4. Brainstorming activity: The child's self-esteem.
5. Building bricks of self-esteem.
6. Follow on thoughts: Activities diary.

1. Discussion of worksheet from Session 3

Ask participants to share their responses to the take home activity from Session 3 -Focus on conflict - communicating feelings. Facilitators can encourage participants to share their ideas and strategies for managing conflicts and developing emotional literacy prior to once again focusing upon the important issue of self-esteem.

2. Introduction

This session aims to review and reinforce the concept of self-esteem previously introduced in session 1. However, the focus here is not primarily upon participant's own self-esteem, but rather on the self-esteem of their children and how this can be further enhanced by those they encounter in all social contexts. Again, the importance of "significant others" in the formulation of personal pictures that people have of themselves is reinforced, alongside the necessity of ensuring positive and constructive feedback which promotes the confidence, emotional literacy, social skills and self-esteem of the children we care for. The activities consequently require participants to identify the characteristics of children who have positive self-esteem and to articulate and put into practice a range of strategies to encourage and promote these positive qualities and attributes.

3. Icebreaker

This Icebreaker can be used as a lead into the activities on children's self-esteem, and is also appropriate for inclusion in workshops for stand-alone sessions on emotional awareness and development in children. The purpose of the activity is to increase participants understanding of the links between communication, self-esteem and confidence and to emphasise the importance of emotional awareness as a key factor in this process.

The facilitator, in introducing the activity, can remind the group that the way people feel about themselves is largely determined by the messages they receive about themselves through communication with other people. Participants should then be asked to find a partner to discuss the following questions:
   * What messages do you get from other people about yourself?
   * What messages do you give your children about themselves?

Bring the group back together and ask each pair to share their responses to the questions, which should be recorded on a flipchart. The range of responses will include both positive and negative messages. Participants may also express strong emotions and feelings stemming from their childhood, relationships and past events. It is important that the facilitator is sensitive to the feelings of group members and if necessary should provide one to one support during or after the session.

The facilitator should advise the group that emotions provide useful feedback and information that can help us to understand ourselves, our children and other people. It can also be pointed out that people's thinking patterns about themselves and situations tend to develop unconsciously, creating a positive or negative self-image.

4. Brainstorming activity: The child's self-esteem. (Worksheet 1)
The aim here is to elicit participant's views regarding evidence of good/positive self-esteem in children -both their own children and other people's children.

Course facilitators can record ideas and responses on a flipchart or participants can make use of the brainstorming sheet provided to record their responses individually or as a member of a pair/small group. If participants decide to work in small groups then it will obviously be necessary to organise a feedback session once ideas have been discussed and recorded. As in previous sessions, it will be interesting to note any similarities, differences, agreements and disagreements as to how children exhibit good self-esteem. Contributions might include some of the following:
   * He/she will generally seem to be outgoing and happy.
   * He/she will be confident.
   * He/she will feel cared for and valued.
   * He/she will like themselves.
   * He/she won't put themselves down.
   * He/she will cope well in view situations/when learning a new concept.
   * He/she will be quite popular.
   * He/she will be able to make and sustain friendships.
   * He/she will be able to take turns and cooperate.
   * He/she will be able to say how they feel about things.
   * He/she won't worry unnecessarily about what others think of them.

5. Building bricks of self-esteem. (Worksheet 2)
The initial brainstorming activity will provide a prompt for the next task which involves participants in identifying ways in which they can further increase their child's/children's self-esteem. This will involve a great deal of discussion and debate in order to generate positive and practical strategies. Participants will be required to reflect on their own behaviours and to highlight the things which have worked for them and their child/children. Ideas proposed may include some of the following:
   * Arrange social situations in which the child can experience success.
   * Praise the child in a meaningful way -not going 'over the top' but sensitively praising good efforts and skills.
   * Take time to listen to the child's views and really listen.
   * Show that you value and care about the child's news and feelings.
   * Criticise in a constructive way.
   * Tell the child that you love and value him/her on a daily basis.
   * Show honest emotions and real, genuine affection towards the child.
   * Allow the child to make choices and to take responsibilities in the home context.

* Ensure the child has access to group activities in which he/she is encouraged to take turns and cooperate.
* Encourage the child to give and receive compliments.
* Help to develop the child's empathy i.e. awareness of other's feelings.
* Encourage the child to participate in new games and activities.
* Regularly highlight and identify positive qualities in both themselves and those around them.

The second part of this activity asks the participants to identify others who may also aid the child in developing positive self-esteem and the strategies that some of these people might use. For example:
* <u>The teacher:</u> He/she will praise the child's work, give them 'special' jobs, encourage cooperative play, set clear boundaries and expectations, will encourage a supportive ethos amongst the peer group, will offer genuine emotional responses and support, etc.
* <u>The Aunty:</u> She'll phone up to say 'well done', she will arrange treats, she will encourage the hobbies, she will make special time to go swimming/watch TV/hold a 'real' conversation.
* <u>Granny:</u> She will take the child shopping, play special games, encourage the child to read, take time to listen, praise and value the child's skills, appearance and personality, etc.
* <u>Brother:</u> He will make 'real' time to sit and listen, to play games, help with homework, read special stories i.e. 'hard' books, play together or with the computer, etc.

What is important in the latter part of the activity is for participants to focus on the child's context and how everyone and everything within that context does, to some extent, impact upon the development of their self-esteem. If your brother constantly fights, argues with you, if your Aunty ignores you, if your Granny continually puts you down and tells you you that are not as clever as your brother/sister, then there will clearly be a negative impact upon the level of confidence and self-esteem that you experience.   Consequently it is essential that parents examine and carefully reflect upon each context and ask appropriate questions such as:
* Does this situation promote my child's self-esteem? How? Why? What can I learn from this?
* Does this situation mitigate against the development of my child's self-esteem? How? Why? What can I learn from this and how can I effect a change for the better?

6. Follow on thoughts: Activities diary. (Worksheet 3)
The final take home activity requires participants to plan one activity for each day of the week which will not only provide the child with a pleasurable experience but will also reinforce and further promote self-esteem. Participants are asked to keep a record of their ideas, the child's responses and their own feelings/reactions on a daily basis for a one-week period. They are then required to reflect upon the activities and to decide which one was the most 'positive' for the child and why this was the case alongside identifying any activities that they feel their child/children may benefit from on a more regular basis.

Example Activities diary

Day	Activity	Child's response	How did you feel?
Sunday	Swimming + water games.	Loved it, very happy, didn't want to leave.	Great to see him so happy. Happy, a bit guilty for not doing it before.
Monday	Reading.	Bit nervous, didn't know words, said 'I'm thick!'	Sorry for him but said it was OK. We'll choose another book.
Tuesday	Game of cards.	Enjoyed it but found it difficult when he lost.	Happy, angry, frustrated.
Wednesday	Watching TV together (Bart).	Loved it, laughter, said 'It is the best'.	A bit irritated, I don't like the programme, but I tried not to show it.
Thursday	Adventure playground.	OK. He enjoyed it and could wait for 1 ride/go.	Happy as he was enjoying it and proud as he didn't push to the front.
Friday	Burger King.	Loved it!!!	Sick!!!
Saturday	Walk in park.	OK for 20 minutes, then said he was cold, could we go home and watch TV?	I loved first 20 minutes. I gave in!

Session 4.   Worksheet 1 Brainstorming activity

Think and discuss! How do you know if a child has good self-esteem? How will they feel, act, think and communicate (both at home and at school)? Record your ideas.

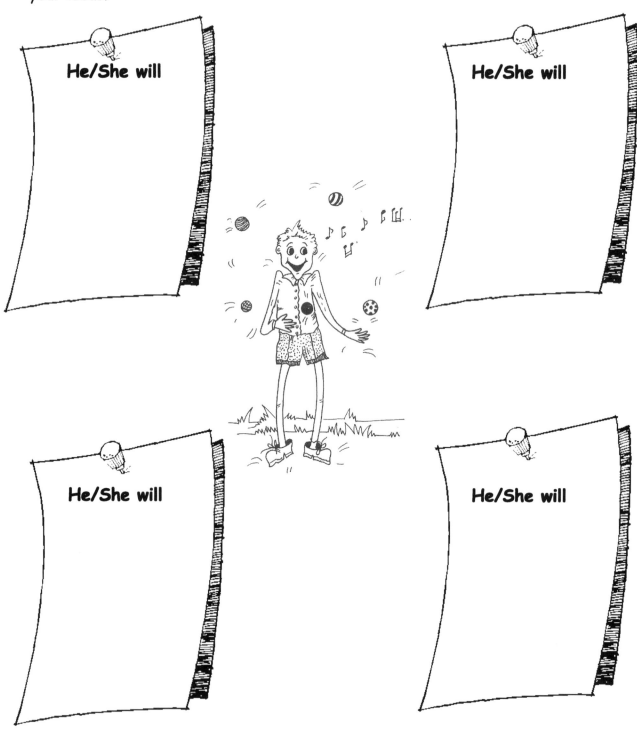

He/She will

He/She will

He/She will

He/She will

Discuss and share your ideas in the group. If your child/children appear not to exhibit all these positive qualities/feelings of well being, discuss and identify the changes that need to be made in order to increase and further promote their self-esteem. What can you do? What can others do? Record your ideas on the reverse of this sheet.

Session 4. Worksheet 2 Building bricks of self-esteem

Identify the ways in which you can further increase your child's self-esteem.
Record your ideas in the building bricks.

Think and reflect! Can anyone else support you in helping your child to feel more
positive? If so, Who? and How? Discuss your ideas and strategies in the group.
Record your ideas on the reverse of this sheet.

Session 4. Worksheet 3 Follow-on thoughts

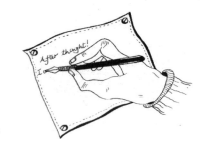

ACTIVITIES DIARY

Plan one activity per day which you know will not only give your child/children pleasure but will also reinforce and further promote self-esteem. Record your ideas and response.

Day	Activity	Child's response	How did you feel?
Sunday			
Monday			
Tuesday			
Wednesday			
Thursday			
Friday			
Saturday			

Think and reflect: Which activity was most positive? Why do you think that this was the case? Are there any activities that you think your child/children might benefit from on a more regular basis? Record your ideas on the reverse of this sheet.

54

Sessions 5
Listening
and Talking

Session 5: Listening and Talking

Group session: 2 hours. This session is divided into 7 sections as follows:

1. Discussion of activities diary from Session 4.
2. Introduction.
3. Ice breaker.
4. Brainstorm: When and why do we need to listen and talk to children?
5. Tips for listening.
6. Ask about yourself.
7. Follow on thoughts: 'Talk time'.

1. Discussion of activities diary from Session 4.
Ask participants to share their responses to the take home activity from Session 4 -Follow on thoughts -Activities Diary. Highlight the activities which reinforced children's positive self-esteem and any similarities between the activities or approaches that participants made use of.

2. Introduction
The ability to actively listen is a skill that is essential for effective communication and valuable in developing relationships. Difficulties and misunderstandings between people, parents and children are often a result of people not listening, or only partially listening or having assumed or misinterpreted what has actually been said.

The activities in this session highlight the difference between hearing which is a physiological process which involves the ears picking up audible sounds and signals and sending them to the brain, and listening which is an intellectual analytical activity involving thoughts and feelings, and is an acquired skill that requires mental effort and energy.

The activities also illustrate the different ways in which people communicate with each other and emphasises the importance of the 'whole' message i.e. the words plus tone of voice, facial expressions, posture and gestures in providing 'meaning' to what is being said.

Participants are encouraged to develop an awareness of the environmental and attitudinal barriers that prevent people from 'really listening' and the effects this can have in the parent-child relationship.

3. Icebreaker
This activity is an introduction to this session on listening and talking. The activity enables participants to experience how it feels not to be listened to and illustrates the importance of both verbal and non-verbal messages in communication.

The facilitator divides the group into two halves and takes one group out of the room. He/She then explains that they will be required to participate in a 2 minute conversation with a member lof the group who has remained in the room. Their partner will be asked to talk about any subject of their choice for 2 minutes whilst they will make it clear (by body language, lack of eye contact, etc.)

that they are not listening. The facilitator should take this group back to the participants who have remained in the room and ask the latter to begin their 2 minute conversation on a topic of their choice.

The participants who were selected to initially remain in the room will find it difficult to talk for 2 minutes without some response or acknowledgement from the other partner. Once everyone has had their turn, the participants should be asked to feedback how they felt. The facilitator can use the following questions to stimulate discussion:
* How did each partner feel when he or she was not being listened to?
* How did it feel to deliberately not listen?
* What did you want to do in each of the situations?
* What did you find yourself doing?
* How can some of the feelings expressed and the obstacles to listening be overcome?

The responses may include:
* Emotions such as: feeling silly, angry, frustrated, not knowing what to say, drying up, distracted, etc.
* Need to have: eye contact, stop talking, touch the other person, get attention, body language, acknowledgement gestures, feedback or non-verbal and verbal responses.

The participants should then be asked to identify the kind of behaviour exhibited by the non-listening partner. The observed behaviour will include some or all of the following:
* No eye contact.
* Fidgeting.
* Preoccupied.
* Distracted.
* Blank or bored expression.
* Looking around the room.
* Yawning.
* Not engaging.
The participants may also suggest additional behaviours.

It should be explained that the first list details how people and children feel when they are not being listened to. The second list is some of the ways in which people can behave when they are not listening.

It should be pointed out that although the list may seem extreme, these behaviours are not as uncommon as we would like to think.

4. Brainstorm: 'When and why do we need to listen and talk to our children? (Worksheet 1)
This activity focuses on communication between parents and children, highlighting the importance of making time and space to listen to and 57talk with children.

The activity gives participants an opportunity to consider how to use open questions when talking with their children and encourage them to express feelings. The facilitator begins the activity by informing the group that several research studies on communication claim that on average the words we use account for only 7% of the messages we send out, tone of voice for 13% and that our body language conveys 80% of the messages we give.

The group should then be asked to divide into smaller groups of three and four and to brainstorm the following questions and list their responses (possible responses are included here).

1. When do children want or need to be listened to?
    * When they come from school.
    * When they are upset or anxious.
    * When they are excited.
    * When they want something.
    * If they need help with homework.

2. When do you find the time to talk with your children?
    * At bed time.
    * During meal time.
    * On the way to and from school.
    * When giving instructions.

3. How do you know if they are listening to you?
    * They do as I say.
    * They reply.
    * Their expression.
    * They ask questions.

4. How do they know if you are 'really' listening to them?
    * They smile.
    * Not sure.
    * Can just tell?

The facilitator can, when discussing the responses, emphasise how difficult it is to 'really' listen and the importance of ensuring that children feel that they are listened to, and are able to talk with ease about their feelings and concerns.

5. Tips for listening. (Worksheet 2)
As a follow on from the brainstorming activity, participants can work individually on worksheet 2 in further considering how we communicate and whether or not they are 'active' listeners. The facilitator may wish to initially highlight how people encode and decode information and provide participants with a definition of 'active listening'.

Participants should rate themselves out of 10 against each of the statements on the list e.g. making special time for listening -I would award myself 5 out of 10 if I felt that I did this every so often i.e. average. If I knew I did this every day, I would award myself 9 or 10 and if I felt that I rarely did this, I might award myself 1 or 2.   Arrange time for feedback and discussion, allowing participants to share and identify their own positive strategies.

6.   Ask about yourself. (Worksheet 3)

Participants will need to complete this activity at home with their child/children and the facilitator may wish to provide time at the start of the next session to allow for feedback. It is important that the group sees this as a positive activity in which they can demonstrate and test their ability to listen to their children and that they can start to identify areas that they would like to improve or change.

7. Follow on thoughts: 'Talk time'. (Worksheet 4)

Again, this final activity is also designed for participants to make use of at home and encourages them to consider ways that they can further help their children to feel positive and develop their own communication skills. This is not designed to be any kind of test (either of the parent or child's skills) but rather as a 'fun' activity. Parents will, however, need to be sensitive in terms of really listening and not attempting to put their own views or words into their children's mouths! It is vital to remember that the children also have the 'right' not to disclose information and to have their own views and ideas heard and listened to.   The activity will also hopefully help participants in identifying specific ways of supporting the child and in building up a bank of resources and ideas for future use e.g. special games, desirable treats, etc.

Session 5. Worksheet 1 Brainstorming Activity

> When and Why do we need to listen and talk to our children?

Think and discuss!

Are there particular times of the day in which children know that you are really listening?

How do you know they are listening to you? Record your ideas on this sheet.

COMMUNICATION

Consider these ideas. Do you feel that you are an 'active listener'? Rate yourself against each top tip and think about how you might further develop your own skills. Give yourself a mark out of 10 at the end of each statement.

TOP TIPS

1. Parents need to make special times for listening when they put everything aside and really focus on listening to what their children have to say. ☐

2. Sometimes a parent can 'shut off' from listening by being bossy/nagging/ giving advice. Try to lessen these behaviours. ☐

3. When a child is upset don't immediately try to give them a solution, let the child talk. Parents should listen and let the child feel understood. ☐

4. Don't just try and console if there is a problem.   This is pretty meaningless and can cause a breakdown in communication. ☐

5. Sometimes just 'listening' can be the solution to a child's problem. ☐

6. Get on the child's level. You can't 'listen' if you are standing over them! ☐

7. Play back the child's feelings e.g. 'I can see you felt bad/upset about that', rather than directly questioning. ☐

8. Ask 'gentle questions' e.g. perhaps, I am not sure but, I wonder if ... etc. ☐

9. Always listen for how the child is feeling, label the feeling and check with the child if you have read the situation correctly. ☐

10. Don't try to correct the child especially when you are feeling angry or upset. Stop and wait until things are calm and try not to use those 4 words: 'I told you so! ☐

Do you agree with these strategies? If so why? If not why not? Are there any other ideas/strategies that have worked for you or your friends? Record your ideas on the reverse of this sheet.

Ask about yourself

Ask your child or partner, adult or friend (if your child is too young) to rate you. Stop and reflect! Can you change anything in order to improve your personal ratings? LISTEN TO YOUR CHILD's responses, let them know that you really value their feedback.

	Bad ☹		OK ☺			Brilliant ☺					
Mark on the scale:	0	1	2	3	4	5	6	7	8	9	10
1. Do I listen to you?											
2. Do I let you make decisions?											
3. Do I show you that I care a lot?											
4. Do I let you have your say?											
5. Do I make special time for you?											
6. Do I help if you have a problem?											
7. Do I praise you?											
8. Do I let you know what you should and shouldn't do? i.e. clear boundaries.											
9. Are my punish-ments fair?											
10. Do I make you feel loved?											

Feedback:
Share feelings on this activity to the group. Can you identify any area that you would really like to change/improve upon?

Session 5. Follow-on-thoughts TALK TIME. (Worksheet 4)

Interview your child!

Listen to his/her responses.

Can you identify any ways that you can further help your child to feel more positive and develop his/her skills?

<u>"Do you need any further help/support in order to do this?"</u>

* Tell me about something good that happened at school today.

* What was your favourite lesson? Why?

* Who did you play with? What did you play?

* Did you do any interesting work? What was it all about?

* How do you feel about the day? Was it happy day, a brilliant day, okay, bad, etc. Why?

* Did you have any problems? If so, what happened? Who helped you? Did you help yourself? What would you do next time if the same thing happened?

* How can I help you? (Listening, solving problems, liaising with teachers and other parents re homework).

* What special games can we play together?

* What would be your favourite weekend treat?

The language may need to be modified or excluded depending on your child's age and needs.

Session 5.   Follow-on-thoughts TALK TIME. (Worksheet 4 continued)

Evaluation of the Interview

What did you notice when you interviewed your child?

What was easy?

Was anything difficult?

How did your child respond?

Other comments.

Session 6
Managing
Challenging
Behaviour

Session 6: Managing challenging behaviour

Group session 2 hours This session is divided into 6 sections as follows:

1. Discussion of two take home activities from Session 5.
2. Introduction.
3. Icebreaker.
4. Brainstorming Activity: What is challenging behaviour?
5. Thinking of real consequences.
6. Follow on thoughts -the Do's and Don'ts of discipline.

1. Discussion of two take home activities from Session 5

Ask participants to share their responses to the take home activities from Session 5 -'Ask About Yourself' and 'Talk Time'. How did participants show that they could 'listen' to their children and develop their communication skills? Can they provide useful ideas and strategies for other members of the group? Have they identified any areas they would like to build upon?

2. Introduction

This session focuses on the concepts of 'unacceptable' and 'challenging' behaviours in both children and adults, and requires participants to consider, formulate and articulate their own personal definitions.

In order to effectively encourage children to develop both responsibility for their own behaviours and the independent skills necessary to manage themselves appropriately in a range of contexts, parents are asked to consider the use and application of 'real' consequences. They are also encouraged to share their own personal methods and strategies alongside considering how and if they can further develop these or introduce and incorporate new ideas and skills. The activities in this session are all designed to promote both reflection and development within a supportive framework. No specific method is presented as the 'right' way to manage challenging behaviour and participants are encouraged to establish what suits them and their children best i.e. that which promotes their happiness, self-esteem, safety and discipline.

3. Icebreaker

This activity introduces the notion of the parent's role in developing independence and responsibility in children. It enables participants to think about their expectations and views about children and what is acceptable and unacceptable behaviour. It should be explained in introducing the activity that these questions should be discussed in terms of the spectrum of responses rather than attempting to reach a consensus on acceptable and unacceptable behaviour.

The facilitator can divide the group into pairs or small groups of three or four to discuss the following questions:
    * What behaviour do you find unacceptable in children?
    * What behaviour do you find unacceptable in adults?
    * What feelings and emotions do they arouse in you?

When each of the pairs or groups have noted down their responses, ask each group to feed back their list of unacceptable behaviour. The facilitator should record on the flipchart the behaviours and feelings that are common to all the groups. Participants discussing these points should be invited to share their reasons for their attitudes and feelings about particular types of behaviour.

To round up the activity, the facilitator recaps on the points raised asking the participants to think back to the activity on models and influences.

4. Brainstorming activity: What is challenging behaviour? (Worksheet 1)

This activity aims to elicit participants' views on what is regarded as unacceptable behaviour in their child/children and children generally. In discussing their views and perceptions, participants will also became aware of some differences between their definitions and those of others. It will be important to focus on the need to listen to each other's views and to accept the very real possibility that we do not share entirely similar social and family values and beliefs. However, it may also became apparent that, despite the differences, there may well be a core set/list of specific behaviours which all participants, regardless of social, cultural and political differences, may share. The basic aim is to describe such behaviours without judging the children or each other! Contributions might include some of the following:
   * Swearing.
   * Shouting back at someone.
   * Hitting others.
   * Unprovoked physical/verbal attacks.
   * Refusal to contribute to household chores.
   * Stealing from parents/friends/family.
   * Spitting.
   * Breaking other's toys/possessions.
   * Lying.
   * Having tantrums.
   * Refusal to go to bed.
   * Refusal to complete homework.
   * Not tidying room.
   * Taking drugs/smoking.
   * Bunking from school.
   * Shoplifting.
   * Bullying, etc.

Participants may want to extend this activity by attempting to rank their list of behaviours in order of seriousness/unacceptability.

5. Thinking of real consequences. (Worksheet 2)

The second activity sheet focuses on the idea that children may be able to learn from the consequences of their own behaviours. This requires participants to consider 'typical' and well used methods of discipline and to compare these to the use of 'real' consequences. 'Real' consequences are those which should result in the child accepting and taking on board the results of his/her behaviours. The example given clarifies this approach: The problem or unacceptable behaviour is that the child is refusing to complete set homework. Typical methods of discipline or attempts to change this behaviour may include a lecture, doing the homework with the child, shouting, moaning, warning, nagging or loss of privileges i.e. sanctions. The use of 'real' consequences might involve the parent(s) in sharing an interest in the homework, asking questions about it and then giving necessary help or letting the child take the consequences for not doing the homework from the teacher e.g. detention, etc.

Participants are asked to discuss and record the 'typical' methods of discipline and the 'real' consequences and their results for the following problems/unacceptable behaviours:
    * Child refuses to go to bed.
    * Child will not help/complete chores in the house.
    * Child has been bullying others at school.
    * Child continually forgets things e.g. packed lunch, homework, P.E. kit, etc.
    * Child is always fighting with younger sibling.
    * Child refuses to turn down music.

Participants should also be asked to provide their own example and to then consciously have a go at using the 'real consequences' method during the coming week. Participants are asked to report back at the next session on their success/otherwise to the rest of the group. It will be important to emphasise that this is one technique amongst many and that it may work better for some children and parents than for others. It is not to be presented as 'the way'/'the right way'. After all, very often the parents are able to find what suits them and each of their individual children best.

6. Follow on thoughts - Do's and don'ts of discipline. (Worksheet 3)
This sheet provides participants with a list of strategies for promoting good discipline and behaviour. It is not designed as a take home activity, as it is a topic which would benefit from group consideration and discussion. Participants should read through the list and then identify (via tick boxes) which strategies they might consider using in the future or that they currently use. The group may add some of their own strategies to the list. Many of the listed strategies will encourage debate amongst the participants which is a necessary part of the process of recognising and articulating beliefs and, identifying what really works for each individual and why. For example:
    * Giving choice and responsibility may be dependent upon the age of the child(ren).
    * Giving a choice may not always be appropriate.
    * Perhaps no one is saint enough to use 'try' instead of 'don't' all the time.
    * There may be times when children need to show anger in a more socially acceptable way.
    * Is it possible not to hit? Is this an out dated method/barbaric/a parental 'right', etc.?

Feedback from this activity will require quality time to enable the group to fully discuss the issues raised. It will certainly not be time wasted. What does continually need to be reinforced though, is the fact that everyone has the right to hold their own beliefs and views on these (and every other) issues and to be respected as individuals.

The idea of focusing on these behaviour management strategies is to highlight similarities and differences and the ways in which parents can and do support each other in coping and dealing with their children's behaviour. Remember - describe and support, don't judge!

Session 6. Worksheet 1 Brainstorming activity

What is
Challenging
Behaviour?
(describe - don't
judge!)

Think and Discuss.
    Are there any significant differences in our own personal definitions?
    Do we share social and family values and beliefs?

Record your ideas on this sheet.

Session 6. Worksheet 2 Thinking of real consequences

Children can learn from the consequences of their own behaviours.
Work together to complete the chart below.

Problem - unacceptable behaviour	Typical methods of discipline	Using real consequences	Results
Child is not doing homework.	Warn, shout, nag, moan, lecture, do homework with	* Show an interest in the homework. * Ask questions, give necessary help. * Let the child take the consequences for not doing the homework from the teacher.	* The child takes on the responsibility for doing homework. * The child develops a relationship with parent.
Child refuses to go to bed			
Child will not help/complete chores in the house.			
Child has been bullying at school.			
Child continually forgets things e.g. packed lunch, homework, P.E. kit.			
Child is always fighting with younger siblings.			
Child refuses to turn down the music.			

Remember! Using 'real consequences' can help to encourage cooperation instead of conflict and defiance. Try it out and report back to the group!

The Do' and Don'ts of Discipline

Look at the suggested strategies. Which do you currently make use of (use the tick box)

☐   Talk things out and listen.

☐   Give choice and responsibility.

☐   Use 'if' instead of 'don't' e.g. 'If you want to use felt-tips, can you put some newspaper down first?' rather than 'Don't use felt-tips on the table!'.

☐   Give and keep clear limits.

☐   Trying not to panic if your child fights against set limits.

☐   Give your child the chance to express his/her feelings of anger and frustration, i.e. let off steam and listen.

☐   Try not to shout, hit, interrupt, swear or criticize.

☐   Encourage your child to express his/her views, i.e. afford respect.

☐   Try to be firm and consistent and do what you said you were going to do.

☐   Encourage children to face and accept the consequences of their own behaviours.

Feedback and discuss your ideas, thoughts and feelings on discipline to the group. Identify which strategies seem to work best and why.

Session 7
Your Child's
Responsibilities

Session 7: Your child's responsibilities

Group session: 2 hours This session is divided into 5 sections as follows:

1. Introduction.
2. Icebreaker.
3. Brainstorming activity: How and when children take responsibility.
4. Responsible parent questionnaire.
5. Follow on thoughts: Self-reflection.

1. Introduction

Enabling children to develop a sense of responsibility for their actions and to find their own solutions to problems can be a challenging and daunting prospect for many parents. Appreciating that our experiences, views and desires may not always be relevant or shared by our children is essential if children are to be encouraged to develop confidence and independence.

The activities in this session focus on the issues of maintaining a balance of power, enabling children to be open and honest whilst at the same time respecting the role of their parents. The activities also enable participants to consider situations when it is appropriate to direct children and when it is more productive to negotiate with children. The session also provides an opportunity for participants to reflect on their own attitudes and behaviour which may contribute positively or negatively to the development of confident, secure and responsible children.

2. Icebreaker

This activity considers some of the stresses and challenges that parents regularly experience and encourages participants to recognise and label stress in themselves and others. Participants explore the possible causes of stress and its impact upon them and their families and how being emotionally self-aware might be useful in the development of coping strategies and positive solutions to conflict situations that may arise in relationships with children.

The facilitator can ask each member of the group to identify two major causes of stress in their current parenting role, and to consider the impact these have had on both themselves and their family. Participants are then asked to work in pairs in order to share their experiences and to identify any similarities and differences in their responses alongside thinking about how they dealt or coped with the situations; i.e. what helped them to cope or what hindered them? The facilitator can then ask the pairs to feedback their responses to the whole group. The key points and recurring themes should be recorded on the flipchart. The list of causes of stress may include the following:

* Getting children to bed.
* Getting children to do as they are told when they are asked.
* Trying to meet all their demands.
* Trying to meet the needs of each child within the family group.
* Constant arguing between siblings.
* Not having enough time to do everything and have quality time.

* Getting children to help around the house.
* Getting children to take responsibility to do their homework.
* Getting children to tidy their rooms.
* Getting children to respect other people and their belongings.
* Not calling home to say where they are and who they are with.
* Not being considerate about telephone use.
* Taking things that don't belong to them.
* Being abusive and disrespectful.
* Violent and aggressive behaviour.
* Not taking care of themselves and abusing their bodies.

When drawing the activity to a close, the facilitator can point out that stress is a condition that affects most people at some point in their lives and although a certain amount can be a good thing, too much can and does result in illness. For parents and carers, factors such as juggling family, home, work and other social demands can place unrealistic expectations and pressures on individuals. There are also internal pressures which people create for themselves, such as the way individuals interpret and deal with their problems, which can also lead to lack of confidence, minimizing their effectiveness in being responsible parents and adults. Should participants identify personal difficulties in this area, the facilitator may (at the end of the session and in confidence), wish to highlight available support agencies.

3. Brainstorming activity: How and when children take on responsibility. (Worksheet 1)
This activity is strongly linked to the activities in session 6, 'managing challenging behaviour'.

The activity provides participants with an opportunity to examine their own attitudes and beliefs about children taking responsibility for their own actions. The facilitator divides the participants into groups of three or four and asks each group to brainstorm the following question from worksheet 1:
* Why is it important for children to take on responsibilities, especially for their own actions?
When the groups have completed the brainstorming exercise, ask each group in turn to feedback their responses and invite the other participants to comment upon these. The facilitator should point out that there is no right or wrong answer, and that the reasons listed all have validity and will have a greater or lesser relevance depending on the age, maturity, needs and circumstances of the child and their family. The following are contributions made by some participants in our groups:
* So that they can learn from their mistakes and successes.
* So that they can adapt to change.
* To enable them to stand on their own two feet.
* To encourage them to be independent.
* To enable them to draw on their own resources and to find solutions for themselves.
* So that they can identify problems and concerns.
* So that they can learn to make choices and decisions for themselves.
* To give them confidence and a positive self-image.
* So that they can become more aware of other needs and situations, i.e. develop more empathy.

The facilitator should point out that the level and range of responsibility parents give children, should be based on their experience and knowledge of them. However, it is also important to be aware of the legal requirements and expectations concerning the appropriate age for children to take on certain responsibilities, e.g. looking after minors, drinking alcohol, consenting to sex, and taking up employment, etc.

4. Responsible parent questionnaire. (Worksheet 2)
In this activity participants continue to explore their attitudes and beliefs. The emphasis is on their responsibility as parents to develop independence and a positive attitude in their children. The activity also looks at the effects of parental attitudes and actions on children's self image and consequent behaviour.

For this activity each participant is given a copy of worksheet 2 (responsible parent questionnaire to complete individually). In groups of three and four, the participants are asked to discuss their responses and to formulate a list of characteristics and approaches that they consider to represent a responsible parent who is able to devolve responsibility, increasing their child's confidence, self-esteem, cooperative skills and sense of responsibility for self.

The facilitator should ask the groups to list down their immediate reactions on flipchart paper. Explain that they should not get 'bogged down' with too much detail at this stage. When the groups have exhausted their ideas, the facilitator should bring the participants together and ask each group to feedback their responses. It may be useful to take one point at a time in order to encourage more in-depth discussion. Participants should be encouraged to clarify their answers and give reasons for the characteristics/approaches they have identified. Responses may include:

* Letting children express themselves.
* Being supportive and encouraging.
* Discussing options and exploring possibilities.
* Letting children learn from their mistakes.
* Not always knowing best.
* Not being overprotective.
* Giving children respect as individuals.
* Listening to and talking with children.
* Encouraging children to ask questions and develop a point of view.
* Not living their lives through their children.
* Offering praise and reward for effort.
* Being honest and sensitive in the feedback you give.
* Accepting that your children's opinions may be different from yours.

The facilitator can point out that the characteristics/approaches listed involve effective communication and an awareness and understanding of the feelings and emotions children experience.

5. Follow-on thoughts - Self Reflection. (Worksheet 3)
This activity is intended for participants to complete individually at home. It is a reflective checklist that enables participants to review and assess the levels and range of responsibility they currently give to their children. It also enables

participants to set targets for increasing the responsibilities they encourage their children to take on. As a note of caution, the facilitator should reassure the group that the activity is not about pushing participants to take action that they are not comfortable with or feel is not right for them at this time. It should be emphasised that not feeling able to encourage children to take on more responsibilities at this time should not be viewed as failure but as recognition of the different needs within the group. Participants can feedback on this activity at the start of the next session.

How and when children take on responsibilities?

Why do you think that it is important for children to take on responsibilities, especially in terms of being responsible for their own actions? Discuss in the group. Record your ideas on the reverse of this sheet.

Session 7. Worksheet 2 Responsible Parents

Responsible parents are those who can and do give their children the opportunity to become responsible. How far do you agree with this statement? Look at the following statements and decide which behaviour would help children to develop responsibility and what would be the effect of the behaviour.

Example

Parent		**Effect on child**
* Is always right	☐ yes	* Argues and lies
* Expects obedience	☑ no	* Fights back
* Has to win		* Doesn't learn any self-esteem

Complete the following:

Parent		**Effect on child**
* Doesn't trust child	☐ yes	*
* Always suspicious	☐ no	*
* Enforces strict rules		*

Parent		**Effect on child**
* Wants perfection	☐ yes	*
* Constantly criticizes	☐ no	*
* Worried about what others will think		*

Parent		**Effect on child**
* Over protective	☐ yes	*
* Shames and spoils	☐ no	*
* Takes over		*

Parent		**Effect on child**
* Gives in all the time	☐ yes	*
* Can't say 'no'	☐ no	*
* Becomes subservient		*

Work in the group to formulate a list of features that you think would describe a responsible parent who is able to devolve responsibility in order to increase their child's confidence, self-esteem, co-operative skills and sense of responsibility for self. Use the back of the page to record your ideas.

Session 7. Worksheet 3 Follow on thoughts. Self Reflect

Things parents might do for their children are listed below. Tick against those tasks which you currently do. Then STOP and THINK! Is your child capable of doing some of the tasks / taking on further responsibility?

☐ Make beds

☐ Get the breakfast

☐ Tidy their rooms

☐ Choose and set out their clothes for the next day

☐ Tidy the toys/clothes, etc.

☐ Lay and clear the table

☐ Wash the dishes and dry up

☐ Sweep the floor / dust around the house

☐ Do their homework with them

☐ Change a plug

☐ Tidy the garden and mow the lawn

☐ Clean windows

☐ Collect the laundry and sort for washing

☐ Do the shopping

☐ Make decisions about their friends

☐ Make decisions about their lives and future

☐ Dress them

☐ Choose and purchase their clothes

TARGET: Set yourself a target for the coming week. Introduce your child / children to 1 new responsibility and monitor progress. Be careful to set a realistic and achievable goal so that your child can really succeed in becoming more responsible. Record your target and progress on the reverse of this sheet.

Session 8
Negotiation
and Control

Session 8: Negotiation and Control

Group session: 2 hours This session is divided into 7 sections as follows:

1. Discussion of follow on thoughts -Self Reflection activity from Session 7.
2. Introduction.
3. Icebreaker.
4. Brainstorming activity: Why discipline?
5. Discipline: Focus on consequences.
6. Consequence cards.
7. Follow on thoughts: Your own consequence cards.

1. Discussion of follow on thoughts -Self Reflection activity from Session 7

Ask participants to share their responses to the take home activity from session 7. Did they recognise that their child was capable of taking on further responsibility? How? When? Did they set any new targets or effect a positive change? Did they find the activity useful?

2. Introduction

This session builds upon the ideas introduced in session 6, particularly focusing upon the concept of "real consequences". Participants are required to consider the need to discipline children and to identify why discipline is or isn't necessary. More time is allocated to considering how useful it is to applyp   82
 real consequences as a form of discipline. Participants are required to question the success of this strategy and the possibility that any strategy or system could be considered successful if it achieves the required results. Participants are given the opportunity to support each other in deciding solutions/strategies for copying effectively with a range of typical discipline problems.

3. Icebreaker

This activity is intended to encourage participants to think about the use of negotiation and control in relationships with both children and other adults. The activity enables participants to explore and identify the processes involved in negotiation and to consider the appropriate uses of control.

For this activity the facilitator should have prepared on a flip chart (but not be shown to the group at this stage) the dictionary definitions of 'negotiation' and 'control'. The concise Oxford Dictionary defines these words as follows: Negotiation: To confer with others in order to reach a compromise or agreement. Control: The power of directing, command. A means of restraint.

The facilitator should divide the participants into groups of 3 and 4 and ask each group to briefly discuss the following questions and to note down their responses on flip chart paper.
    * What is negotiation?
    * What does it involve?
    * When is it most appropriate to negotiate?
    * What is control?
    * What does it involve?
    * When is it most appropriate to make use of control?

Each group should then be asked in turn to present their responses which may include the following phrases and words:

Negotiation	Control
bargaining	managing
discussing	limiting
agreeing	restricting
debating	opposing
compromise	power
finding a way through	restraint.
resolving difficulties.	

The facilitator should encourage participants to give explanations for their responses to the appropriate uses of negotiation and control. When all the views of the group have been exhausted the facilitator should then present to the group the prepared definitions of negotiation and control. The facilitator can highlight the similarities between the responses listed by the group and the general definition found in the dictionary.

4. Brainstorming activity: Why discipline? (Worksheet 1)

The aim of this brainstorming activity is to elicit participants' views as to why parents 'need' to discipline their children. The discussion will, most probably, also include issues regarding power within the family relationship, the necessity of maintaining a balance of power and some kind of evaluation as to where discussion and negotiation enter into this process. Initially, this activity might best be done in the whole group with course facilitators recording responses and ideas. However, if participants decide to work in smaller groups, then it will obviously be necessary to organise a feedback session once ideas have been discussed and recorded. As in previous sessions, it will be interesting to note any similarities, differences, agreements and disagreements as to why participants think discipline is necessary or otherwise. Contributions might include some of the following:

* In order to maintain a balance of power.
* To keep some level of 'peace' in the home.
* To teach what is right/wrong/good/bad.
* So they behave appropriately outside the home, i.e. Don't embarrass me!
* So that they don't grow up to be selfish and self-centred.
* So that they know their behaviours have consequences, e.g. you break a window, you pay for a replacement.
* To show the child that you have to 'pay' for doing wrong.
* They need to respect others and you can only do so through being disciplined about allowing others to have their rights.
* Children need to learn socially acceptable behaviour through discipline. If you can't then you won't be able to keep a job/cope in school.
* They need to know that they don't run things and that everyone has a say and everyone has their own needs.

5. Discipline: Focus on consequences. (Worksheet 2)

Session 6 introduced the idea of using 'real' consequences and this is revisited here, with more time to focus on this strategy and question how successful it may or may not be, participants should also be prompted to question whether or not any system is 'right' for everyone or if any system is okay as long as it gets the required results.

The focus on consequences sheet describes a specific scenario in which young children can be seen arguing and bickering in front of the television. The parent does not nag or shout at the children but simply says "I can't stand this noise. Either you stop arguing or go outside / next door and miss the programme." If the children continue to argue and bicker then it is suggested that they have made the choice to leave the room. The parent may wish to provide them with a further choice, i.e. to behave or be carried out and then to be allowed to return to the room once they have made up their minds to watch the programme sensibly.

It may be that some participants do make use of such a strategy whilst others do not feel that it is appropriate for their child/children. What is important is that this scenario is used to prompt debate and it is suggested that making use of the questions could provide a helpful framework for the discussion itself. In discussing whether the approach is useful or realistic, participants may identify a range of their own personal strategies which they have found useful. This 'sharing' process should be seen as supportive as participants will need to feel safe in highlighting any personal difficulties if they are to gain real, practical support from the group as a whole.

6. Consequence cards. (Worksheet 3)

This activity again requires participants to 'brainstorm' solutions to specific behaviour problems and to work together as a group in order to come to some agreement as to the proposed approach. It may well be that more than one approach is deemed to be of use or appropriate and these can be recorded on the reverse of the cards. Participants may wish to work on this activity in smaller groups or pairs, with one member of the group acting as a scribe. Time should be allocated for feedback to the whole group on completion of the consequence cards. The problems indicated on the cards are designed to reflect real-life situations. However, if during the course of these sessions, participants have highlighted other problems which they would be happy to share in the group, then these can be recorded on blank consequence cards and used in place of the set activity.

The consequence cards describe the following problems:
* Child throws a tantrum in the shop when you refuse to buy a toy.
* Child throws a tantrum at home when not allowed to stay up late.
* Child won't get out of bed in the morning.
* Child refuses to do homework.
* Child stays out for 2 hours over the set limit.
* Child hits another child and this is an unprovoked attack witnessed by you.
* Child plays on computer instead of doing homework.
* Child refuses to talk to parent because he/she didn't get own way about bed-time.
* Child refuses to eat any vegetables at all.
* Child continually teasing and taunting younger brother.
* Child refuses to share toys with sister.
* Child breaks sister/brother's toy because he/she was in a bad mood.
* Child steals money from your purse.

* Child dressing outrageously and sent home from school.
* Child refuses to baby-sit for younger sibling saying 'I'm not your servant'.

These consequence cards are presented on four worksheets with four problems detailed on each sheet. Participants can be provided with one sheet each and record responses on the reverse of the sheet. It would obviously be helpful if each of the smaller subgroups worked on the same consequence card sheet.

7. Follow-on thoughts. Your own consequence cards. (Worksheet 4)

The final activity aims to encourage participants to make use of the consequence cards in their own home environment. The blank cards provided here allow for each parent to identify personal problems that they have observed or experienced and to work with a partner/close relative in order to form and record the consequences they feel to be appropriate for these behaviours on the reverse of each card. Again, this process will engender some debate and participants will need to again recognise that there may not be agreement between each person as to the best or most positive approach. This may also raise further issues as to how and if there is a need to come to some agreement in regards to methods of discipline in order to ensure a consistent approach from all members of the family group. It may be useful to allow feedback on this particular activity to the group as a whole at the start or end of the next session.

Think and discuss! Why do parents need to discipline their children? What kind of discipline is needed in order to maintain a balance of power? Where does discussion and negotiation enter in to this process?

Session 8.   Worksheet 2 Discipline: Focus on consequences

Is a system of punishment and rewards effective? Or, do children need to learn to take responsibility for their own behaviours and actions?

<u>Scene:</u>
Youngish children are arguing and bickering in front of the TV. Parent does not nag/shout but says 'I can't stand this noise. Either you stop arguing or go outside/ next door and miss the programme.' If the children continue, then they have made their choice, i.e. to leave the room! A further choice can also be given 'do you want to leave or shall I carry you out - you can come back in when you have made up your minds to watch sensibly?'

Questions to consider. Discuss in the group!

1. Is this approach realistic?

2. Does it encourage more responsibility?

3. Does it encourage more negotiation and increase the child's awareness of the consequences of certain behaviour?

4. Is this a 'firm' approach?

5. Does the child/children know that the parent has, in fact, taken control of discipline?

6. Do you have any suggestions as to other methods of discipline? Can you suggest how and why these might also be effective?

7. Finally, is our system 'right' for everyone or is any system okay as long as it gets results? What would be a negative method of disciplining children?

Record your ideas on the reverse of this sheet.

Session 8. Worksheet 3 Consequence cards

Look at the discipline problems detailed on the consequence cards. Discuss what the consequences of these behaviours might/should be and how you might implement them.

Record your responses and then share your ideas within the group. Is there any agreement? Does there appear to be a 'best' or most positive approach?

Child throws a tantrum in the shop when you refuse to buy a toy.

Child throws a tantrum at home when not allowed to stay up late.

Child won't to get out of bed in the morning.

Child refuses to do homework.

Session 8. Worksheet 3 Consequence cards

Look at the discipline problems detailed on the consequence cards. Discuss what the consequences of these behaviours might/should be and how you might implement them.

Record your responses and then share your ideas within the group. Is there any agreement? Does there appear to be a 'best' or most positive approach?

Child stays out for two hours over the set limit.

Child hits another child and this is an unprovoked attack witnessed by you.

Child plays on computer instead of doing homework.

Child refuses to talk to parent because he/she didn't get own way about bed time.

Session 8.   Worksheet 3 Consequence cards

Look at the discipline problems detailed on the consequence cards. Discuss what the consequences of these behaviours might/should be and how you might implement them.

Record your responses and then share your ideas within the group. Is there any agreement? Does there appear to be a 'best' or most positive approach?

Child refuses to clean bathroom/ complete a chore around house.

Child refuses to eat any vegetables at all.

Child continually teasing and taunting younger brother.

Child refuses to share toys with sister.

Session 8. Worksheet 3 Consequence cards

Look at the discipline problems detailed on the consequence cards. Discuss what the consequences of these behaviours might/should be and how you might implement them.

Record your responses and then share your ideas within the group. Is there any agreement? Does there appear to be a 'best' or most positive approach?

Child dressing outrageously and sent home from school.

Child steals money from your purse.

Child breaks sister/ brother's toy because he/ she was in a 'bad' mood.

Child refuses to baby-sit for younger sibling saying 'I'm not your servant.'

**Session 8. Worksheet 4 Follow on thoughts:
Your own consequences cards**

Make up your own cards, identifying own discipline problems you have observed/
experienced. Work with a partner/close relative in family and recording the
consequences of these behaviours on the reverse of the cards. Can you agree?
Can you identify a more positive approach?

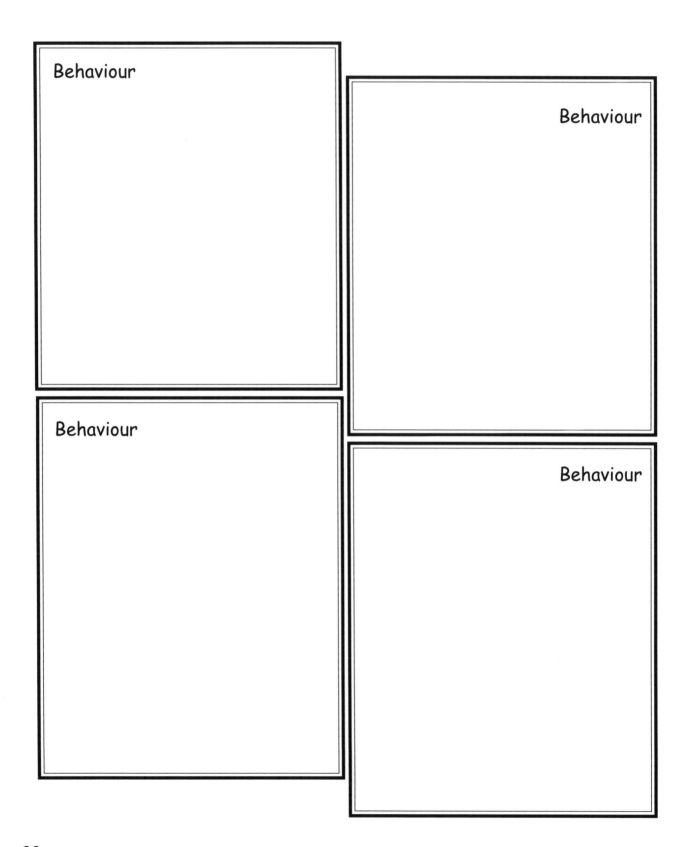

Session 9
Working in
Partnership with
the School

Tina Rae

Session 9: Working in partnership with the school

Group session: 2 hours This session is divided into 6 sections as follows:

1. Discussion of take home activity from Session 8 -Your own consequence cards.
2. Introduction.
3. Icebreaker.
4. Brainstorming activity: Working in partnership with the school.
5. Learning and teaching together.
6. Follow on thoughts: Focus on behaviour.

1. Discussion of take home activity - Your own consequence cards.

Ask participants to share their responses to the take home activity from Session 8. Ask the group to present their consequence cards and to identify positive responses. Are there significant agreements and similarities? Can participants agree on 'positive' responses?

2. Introduction

The session focuses on the important role parents have in helping their children's development and learning and that by working together with the school or pre-school setting they become joint educators and create a strong partnership of support. The activities enable participants to consider the meaning of partnership with the school and the role of parents, pupils, school staff and governors in achieving a supportive working relationship, in which children feel confident and able to achieve and parents feel included in their child's learning. The activities in this session are strongly linked to session 8, but can be used for workshops and stand-alone sessions on home/school partnerships and parental involvement.

3. Icebreaker

The purpose of this activity is to raise participants' awareness of how feelings are a very important part of communication and that through both verbal and non-verbal behaviour, people send out messages about how they feel about themselves and other people.

This activity should be introduced by asking participants to think of three or four different social situations perhaps talking to a child, their child's teacher, a friend, or meeting someone for the first time. The participants are then asked to brainstorm in pairs or in groups of three and four, thoughts or feelings that they might experience in these situations which may prevent them from listening. Each group or pair should record their responses on flipchart paper. It may be helpful for the facilitator to provide an example from their own experience to initiate responses from the group. The facilitator should then bring the small groups together and ask each group in turn to present their brainstorming list. There will be a number of similarities and some differences, which can be highlighted to emphasis the range of thought and feeling barriers and how common a reaction it is not to listen. The thoughts and feelings that may be expressed from the group are:

* Thinking about how to respond.
* Being anxious about other things.
* Wanting to make a good impression.
* Wanting to advise the other person and give a good solution.
* Making judgements about the person, positively or negatively.
* Thinking about what they are going to do next.
* Thinking about their own situation.
* Whether or not they can relate to what is being said.
* Not having the time to spare.
* Triggers off other thoughts.
* Making assumptions about what you think the person is going to say.

The facilitator can explain that the examples of barriers to listening identified, happen more frequently than we would like to believe in everyday conversations with both adults and children. Unless people make a conscious effort to actively listen, it is very easy to become distracted and preoccupied with other thoughts. It is also important to be aware of the feelings and emotions that are aroused by what is being said and that people communicate using a combination of senses.

4. Brainstorming activity: Working in partnership with the school. (Worksheet 1)

This activity is designed to start participants thinking about what is meant or intended by 'partnership with the school' and what this implies for them as parents. The activity also enables participants to identify ways in which they can encourage their child's learning and development, and the information and support schools can provide.

In introducing the activity, the facilitator can present to the group a definition of 'partnerships' and discuss briefly the concept in general terms. Such definitions might be as follows:
* The state of being a partner or partners.
* A joint business.
* A pair or group of partners.
* A joint enterprise with equal responsibility for productivity/outcomes.
* Mutual respect.
* Complementary expertise.
* A willingness to learn from each other.

The participants are then asked to divide into groups of threes and fours and to brainstorm recording their responses on flipchart paper, the following questions from worksheet 1.

* What is meant by working in partnership with the school?
* How can I support my child's learning and development?
* What are my expectations of the school in this process?

When the groups have all completed this exercise, the facilitator should go through each question asking each group to present their responses and invite comments and questions from the other participants. The facilitator should point out that the range of responses illustrates many different expectations that people have. The group will tend to include the following words in their definition of partnership:

equal	balanced/shared
valuing	partners
joint	corporation
together	mutual
agreement	united.

The following responses may be listed for supporting children's learning and development:

* Helping with homework.
* Involving them in out of school activities.
* Learning through everyday activities i.e. cooking, shopping, playing, etc.
* Reading together.
* Going on outings and trips.
* Helping out in school.
* Developing one's own skills.
* Knowing how to help the child.

The typical responses to what your expectations of the school may include:

* Information on how to help with homework.
* Information on support groups and services that are available to help families.
* Staff listening to parents and treating all parents with respect.
* The school starting from the premise that parents want to be supported.
* Respect and valuing what parents know about their children.
* Including parents in decisions about their children and the school generally.
* Being told positive things about their child.
* Knowing what the school policies and rules are.
* Being clear about what the school expects from parents.
* Staff being honest and open.
* All children being valued and treated fairly regardless of race or special need.

Participants should be advised when all the points are being discussed that schools will also have expectations about the responsibilities of parents which will partly be guided by government legislation and requirements and partly by the culture and the ethos of the particular school such as; attendance, punctuality, support with homework and reading and behaviour, etc. It should also be pointed out that parents should ensure that they are aware of where they can obtain the relevant information.

5. Learning and teaching together. (Worksheet 2)
This activity is intended to help participants review the extent to which they are currently involved in supporting their children's learning. It also enables participants to identify school policies and processes that are essential information for understanding the responsibilities of the school and the home in the education of children. The activity starts with a quick check in the group to establish whether all group members have been or are involved in their children's learning and to draw out views about parental inclusion in schools.

The facilitator then provides a copy of worksheet 9.2 self-checklist and asks each participant to first indicate their current level of involvement, any areas of concern or where they require more information against the checklist. Participants should then make a personal action plan listing the changes they would like to make in terms of their involvement and relationship with the school and to think about how they will go about achieving this.

Participants are then asked to share their action plans in groups of three and four and to consider how they can support each other in further developing positive relationships with schools.

6.   Follow-on thoughts: Focusing on behaviour. (Worksheet 3)

This activity is designed to be a take home sheet. The activity enables participants to identify the strategies and approaches used in dealing with challenging behaviour and for encouraging positive self-esteem in children. Participants are further encouraged to compare their methods with that of the school.

Participants are given a copy of worksheet 3 to be completed at home.   They are asked to complete the reflection boxes as directly and honestly as possible. The group should be advised that if they have difficulty in completing the exercise, they might find it helpful to arrange to meet with a member of staff from the school who can provide them with the relevant information.

Session 9. Worksheet 1 Working in partnership with the school
Brainstorming activity

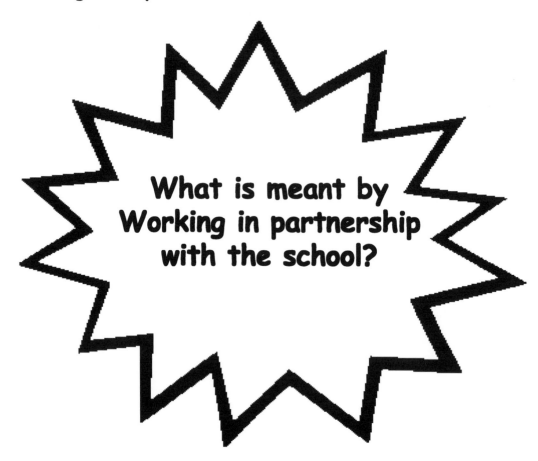

What is meant by
Working in partnership
with the school?

Think and discuss! Record your ideas on this sheet.

* What does this mean?

* How can you support your child's learning and development?

* What are your expectations of the school in this process?

* Can we agree definitions?

Session 9. Worksheet 2 Learn and teach together

How can you participate in this process? Look at the checklist below in order to determine the extent to which you are currently involved in your child's education.

Self-check	Yes	No
I know how the school teach literacy and numeracy skills and I am able to support my child at home in these areas.	☐	☐
I can discuss my child's progress when I need to.	☐	☐
I can ask school staff for advice.	☐	☐
I understand how the school's policies on behaviour management and bullying work.	☐	☐
I am aware of the school's SEN Policy and how they provide the inclusion of children with SEN.	☐	☐
I feel that school staff will listen to any concerns I have and then follow them up.	☐	☐
I am aware how the school rewards children for good work and good behaviour.	☐	☐
I know what the school regards as acceptable behaviour.	☐	☐
I agree with the school's definitions of 'good' behaviour.	☐	☐
I think that the school staff consider me to be supportive of their efforts on behalf of my child.	☐	☐

ACTION PLAN

STOP!   Do you have any concerns regarding your responses?

THINK!   Can you think of ways you might be of more help to the teachers? Do you need more information?

PLAN!   Make an action plan. Identify the changes that you would like to make / areas to develop further and how you can go about this in the most positive way.

Record your action plan on the reverse of this sheet.

Session 9. Worksheet 3 Follow-on thoughts.
Focus on behaviour

One area in which parents can particularly work in partnership with the school is in promoting appropriate behaviours and positive attitudes.

Try to complete the following questions.

<u>Record your views on the reverse of this sheet.</u>

If you have any concerns/difficulties/are unaware of school's policies in any of these areas, arrange to meet with a member of staff and involve them in this process.

<u>Consider and reflect</u>

1. What do you consider to be good behaviour?	What does the school consider to be good behaviour?	How do your views compare?
2. How do you raise the self-esteem of your child?	How do staff raise the self-esteem of your child?	How do your views/ strategies compare?
3. What are your sanctions and methods for coping with inappropriate behaviour?	What are the school's sanctions and methods with coping with inappropriate behaviour?	How do your views/ strategies compare?
4. How do you support the school in promoting the self-esteem and good behaviour of your child?	How does the school support you in promoting the self-esteem and good behaviour of your child?	How do your views/ strategies compare?

<u>Remember!</u>

Consistency can be a key to success.

Are there any ways you can work on further developing a consistent approach?

Talk to the teacher!

Feedback your findings, views and ideas to the group in the next session.

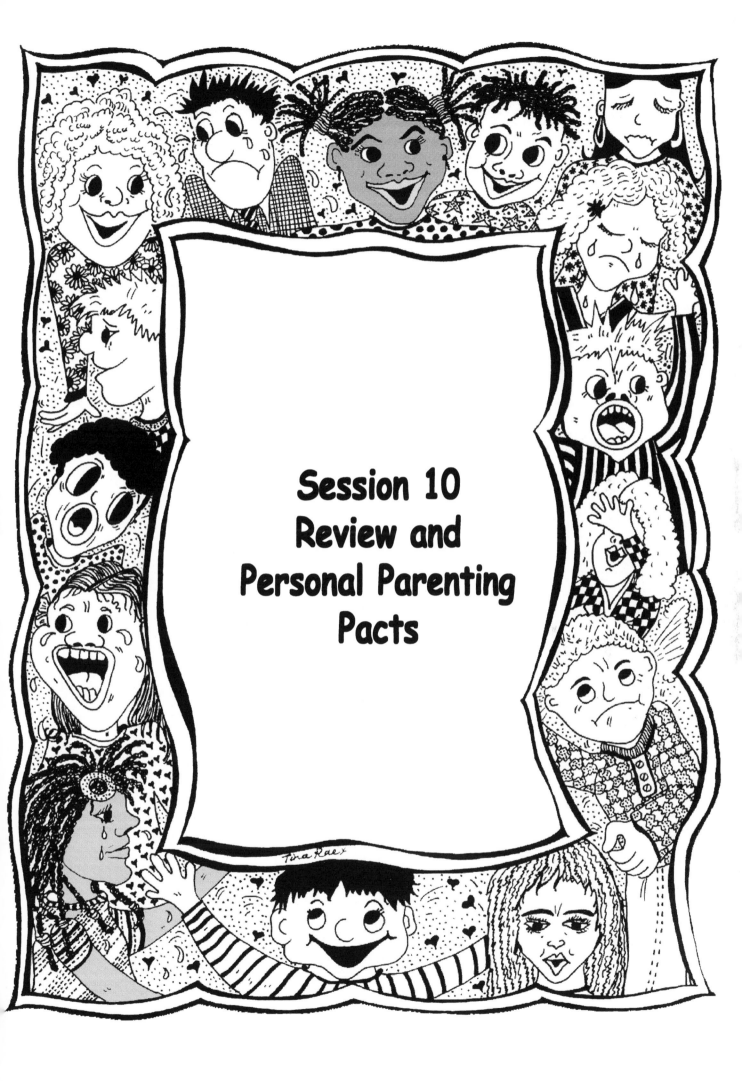

Session 10
Review and
Personal Parenting
Pacts

Session 10:   Review and personal parenting pacts

Group session: 2 hours This session is in 6 sections as follows:

1. Discussion of the take home activity from Session 9 - Follow on thoughts - Focus on Behaviour.
2. Introduction.
3. Icebreaker.
4. Brainstorming activity: How can we be positive parents?
5. Self evaluation checklist: Reflection and evaluation.
6. Follow on thought: Action plan.

1. Discussion of the take home activity - Focus on Behaviour.

Ask participants to share their responses to the take home activity from Session 9. Focus particularly on how group members can work with the school or pre-school setting in order to develop a consistent and agreed approach to these issues. It may also be helpful to highlight and then brainstorm any particular difficulties that may be raised.

2. Introduction

The activities in this session reflect on the earlier sessions and are intended to assist participants in reviewing how the programme has enabled them to meet some of the individual and group learning goals identified at the beginning of the programme. Bringing together the programme in the review and action planning session can be an empowering experience for the group, enabling individuals to recognise the skills and understanding they currently have and bring to their parenting role. It can be a confidence booster, making participants feel that they are capable of positive parenting. Group members will also be able to identify aspects of their parenting which they would like to further develop.

The facilitator should ensure that the programme ends on a positive note, as it is essential that the group members feel confident and able to utilise the skills, knowledge and strategies that they have acquired, and to continue to build upon them.

3. Ice breaker. (Worksheet 1)

This activity is intended to help participants identify the support networks available to them in their everyday relationships with family, friends, neighbours, work colleagues as well as available support services and agencies. It is also helpful in getting participants to develop an awareness of the groups, services and agencies that provide activities, information, advice and support to parents.

Participants should first be asked to individually map out the people and organisations who they know they can rely on for advice and practical support, starting with themselves in the centre and working outwards to illustrate the level of support or significance of the persons or organisations involved. Participants should be provided with worksheet 1 for this purpose. When all group members have completed this exercise, the facilitator should bring together the responses, listing on the flipchart the range of services, groups and agencies identified in order to create a resource and reference list for the whole group. For some participants this will be very necessary information that will enable them to meet the current and future needs of their children and families more effectively.

Participants may raise positive and negative issues about individuals or groups within their network. They may identify their supporters as:

Negative	Positive
* Inclined to take over	* They are always there for me
* Can not maintain confidence	* They listen and encourage me
* Can be biased or prejudiced	* They will provide practical help
* Judgemental and critical	* They take a balanced view
* I told you so ...	* They don't judge me
* Have their own problems	* I can trust them to keep my confidence
* Have very rigid and set views and expectations.	* I don't owe them anything in exchange.

Participants will, in considering both the positive and negative aspects of support, touch upon cultural, religious and social influences that have an impact on the availability and extent of their support network. These issues should be handled carefully to ensure that group members are not left feeling vulnerable or alienated from their support networks.

4. Brainstorming activity: How to be positive parents? (Worksheet 2)

In introducing this activity the facilitator may find it useful to recap on main or key issues covered in the programme to date. It may be helpful to have reviewed the information recorded on the flipcharts from each of the previous sessions before this session, and to have noted down key issues, themes, strategies and information points.

Participants should then be asked to individually note down the main ways in which they feel they can support their child in developing the confidence, emotional awareness, self-esteem and behavioural coping strategies they will need in order to survive and succeed in school and in social relationships.

When all group members have completed this part of the activity, the facilitator should then divide the group into pairs and ask participants to share their responses, listing down similarities and differences.

The participants are then asked to evaluate their progress against their initial learning goals which were identified at the beginning of the programme.

Group members should hopefully be able to notice some change and development in their attitudes and ability to support and encourage their children in developing positive self-esteem, confidence and independence.

Participants may have also identified areas of personal growth in themselves, which may include:
* Being more confident.
* Being less anxious about their role as a parent.
* Dealing better with conflicts between themselves and their children.
* Having a more positive outlook.
* Feeling less isolated.
* Understanding their children better.
* Being aware of more strategies they can use.
* Feeling more assertive.
* Interested in further learning or training.
* Feeling more comfortable speaking in groups.
* More awareness of their own feelings and how these impact upon others.

5. Self-evaluation checklist: Reflection and evaluation. (Worksheet 3)
This activity provides an opportunity for participants to reflect upon and evaluate their achievements through a series of statements that refer to their own understanding, emotional awareness and development of self-esteem alongside their children's development in these key areas.

Participants should be asked to tick the appropriate boxes on the worksheet which should be provided for each group member. They are then asked to rate themselves from A to C in terms of their achievements in each category. This activity should be used as a personal development tool and as a measurement of participants' progress and achievements throughout the programme. Participants should be encouraged to answer the statements as honestly and directly as possible, as this will provide them with a self assessment which will enable them to set new goals and targets for themselves.

6. Follow on thought: Personal parenting pacts
Participants should identify new learning targets and goals from the previous activity for themselves and, if appropriate, for their children. These do not have to be shared with the group as they are for participant's personal use in the future. The following questions may be helpful to participants in developing an action plan and will also be important feedback for the facilitator.

* What I want to know and skills I want to develop?
* What I have learnt about myself?
* What I have learnt about my children?
* What I have learnt about my relationship with my family?
* What changes would I like to make about the way I do things?
* What I would like to change about the way we do things?
* What other actions would I like to take?
* What have been the positive things for me through the programme?
* What else would I have liked the course to include?

The conclusion to the programme is important as it should enable group members to recognise skills and understanding that they have developed both individually and as a group. If group members feel confident and capable, they will also feel empowered to further build and maintain positive relationships with their children. Their skills, confidence and self-esteem should have increased so as to hopefully have a positive effect on their own behaviours and those of the children and adults within their lives and social contexts.

It is vital that facilitators arrange for a celebration at the end of this final session. This could include the facilitator giving a brief summary of the skills, knowledge and strategies that parents have developed during the course alongside presenting a certificate of completion and providing appropriate refreshments! Whatever the type or content of this celebration, it is important that parents' hard work and commitment is both recognised and rewarded. It is equally important that their increasing confidence, skills and self-esteem are clearly acknowledged. A positive ending should hopefully aid the promotion of positive new beginnings.

Session 10. Worksheet 1 My Support Network

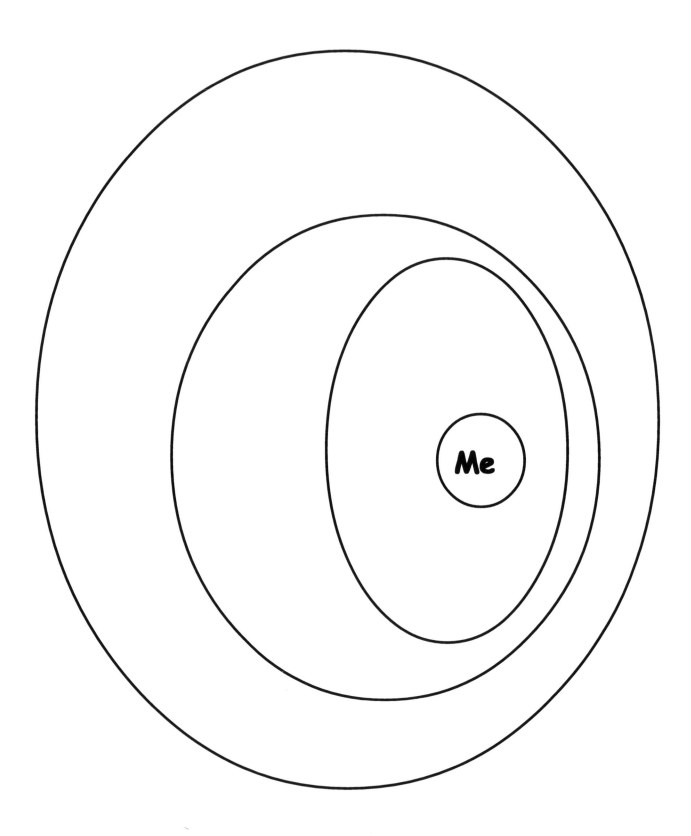

Using the above diagram, write down the name of people e.g. partner, parent, friends, or agencies e.g. school, Social Services, etc. who form your support network. Use the inner circles to illustrate those closest and most supportive to you.

How can we be "Positive Parents"?

Think back and reflect on the previous sessions! What are the main ways in which we can support our children in developing the confidence, emotional aware-ness, self-esteem and behavioural coping strategies that they will need in order to succeed?

Record your ideas on this sheet.

Session 10. Worksheet 3 Reflect and evaluate! Focus on you!

Look at the achievements list and tick against the statements which apply to you:

a. mostly   b. sometimes   c. rarely.

I am aware of what it means to have good self-esteem.   a ☐ b ☐ c ☐

My self-esteem is okay.   a ☐ b ☐ c ☐

My child's self-esteem is okay.   a ☐ b ☐ c ☐

I am aware of the main models and influences on my parenting style.   a ☐ b ☐ c ☐

I have a clear idea of what I think a 'good' parent is.   a ☐ b ☐ c ☐

I understand my own emotional triggers.   a ☐ b ☐ c ☐

I understand my child's emotional triggers.   a ☐ b ☐ c ☐

I feel that I can make my child feel loved and valued on a daily basis.   a ☐ b ☐ c ☐

I can cope reasonably effectively with my anger.   a ☐ b ☐ c ☐

I feel reasonably confident in dealing with my child's strong emotions.   a ☐ b ☐ c ☐

I can identify a child whose self-esteem is fragile.   a ☐ b ☐ c ☐

I understand how I can increase self-esteem in a child via my own behaviours and responses.   a ☐ b ☐ c ☐

I can be an 'active listener'.   a ☐ b ☐ c ☐

I can ask 'gentle questions'.   a ☐ b ☐ c ☐

I can listen out for my child's feelings.   a ☐ b ☐ c ☐

I try not to nag or boss.   a ☐ b ☐ c ☐

I can make time to talk.   a ☐ b ☐ c ☐

I have a clear idea as to what is unacceptable behaviour.   a ☐ b ☐ c ☐

I can make use of consequences in order to encourage co-operation instead of conflict.　　a ☐　b ☐　c ☐

I can allow my child to express feelings and opinions and to make certain choices.　　a ☐　b ☐　c ☐

I can be firm and stick to my guns!　　a ☐　b ☐　c ☐

I understand the distinction between a 'responsible' parent and one who does not foster responsibility in the child.　　a ☐　b ☐　c ☐

I recognise behaviours which help children to develop responsibility.　　a ☐　b ☐　c ☐

I can make use of behaviours which help children to develop responsibility.　　a ☐　b ☐　c ☐

I recognise the tasks that my child is capable of doing.　　a ☐　b ☐　c ☐

I am happy to introduce new responsibilities step by step.　　a ☐　b ☐　c ☐

I understand why there is a need for discipline.　　a ☐　b ☐　c ☐

I have gained confidence in setting clear boundaries.　　a ☐　b ☐　c ☐

I can use consequences when disciplining my child.　　a ☐　b ☐　c ☐

I feel reasonably confident that I have developed my skills in disciplining my child.　　.　　a ☐　b ☐　c ☐

I can negotiate with my child effectively, without feeling that I have lost control.　　a ☐　b ☐　c ☐

I feel confidentto work in 'partnership' with the school.　　a ☐　b ☐　c ☐

I feel comfortable with the way in which the school manages behaviour.　　a ☐　b ☐　c ☐

I feel comfortable with the way in which the school promotes each individual's self-esteem.　　a ☐　b ☐　c ☐

I think that school staff see me as a supportive parent.　　a ☐　b ☐　c ☐

I think I am a POSITIVE PARENT!　　a ☐　b ☐　c ☐

Session 10. Worksheet 4 Personal Parenting Pacts

Stop and think. Look right back! Refer to your initial scaling activity. How did you rate yourself on the scale? How positive did you feel about your skills? What has changed since then? Also, refer to the final 'Focus on you!' Quiz. Are there any areas you would like to change/develop further? What do you now need to do in order to become an even more positive parent?

Once you have reflected on these questions, try to complete your own PERSONAL PARENTING PACT.

I will make a pact with myself and my family to work on the following skills:

1.

2.

3.

I will ask my friends to help me by:

I will ask my child/children to help me by:

I will ask partners and relatives to help me by:

I will review my own progress in [   ] weeks on [   ]

FINALLY-A-DECLARATION! I will not aim to be a 'perfect parent' but I will aim to be a 'positive parent'.

Signed _____Date: _____

Witnessed by my supportive friends and family _____

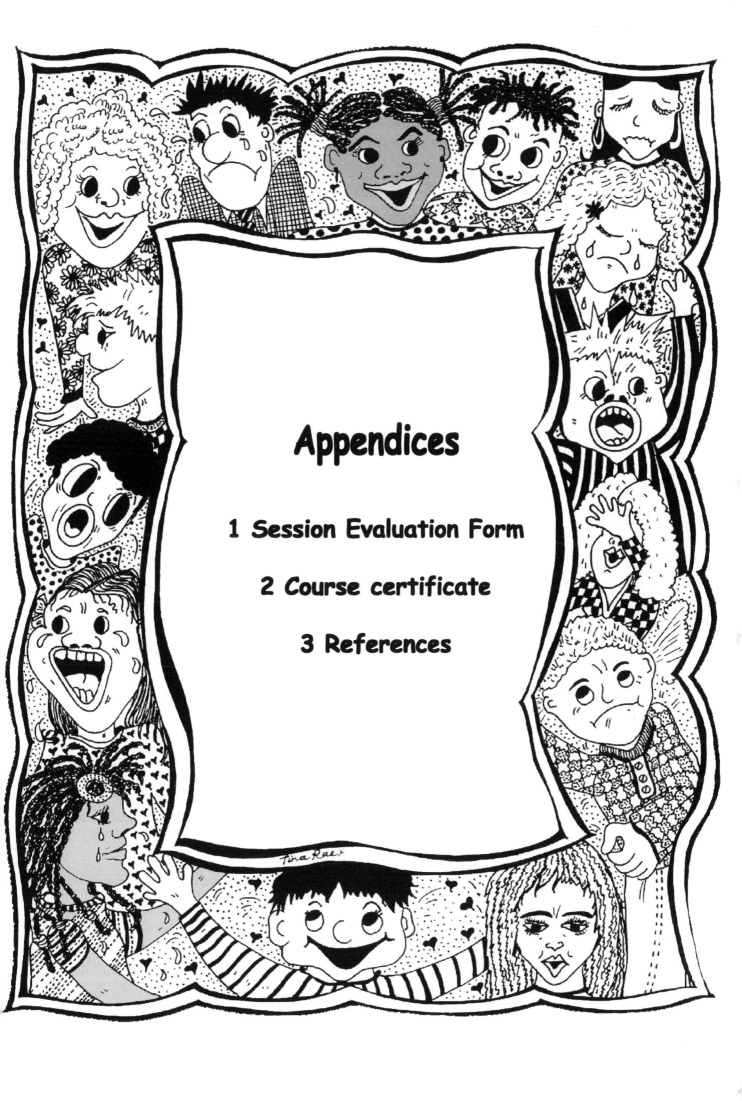

Appendices

1 Session Evaluation Form

2 Course certificate

3 References

Developing Parenting Skills, Confidence and Self-esteem.

Session Evauation Form   **Session number** _____

Please complete the following questions:

1. What did you think of today's session

2. What did you find most useful?

3. Would you have liked to cover different points - please describe.

4. What do you think you gained from the session?

5. Overall would you rate the session as

Excellent ☐ Very good ☐ Good ☐ Satisfactory ☐ Poor ☐

Thank you for your help.

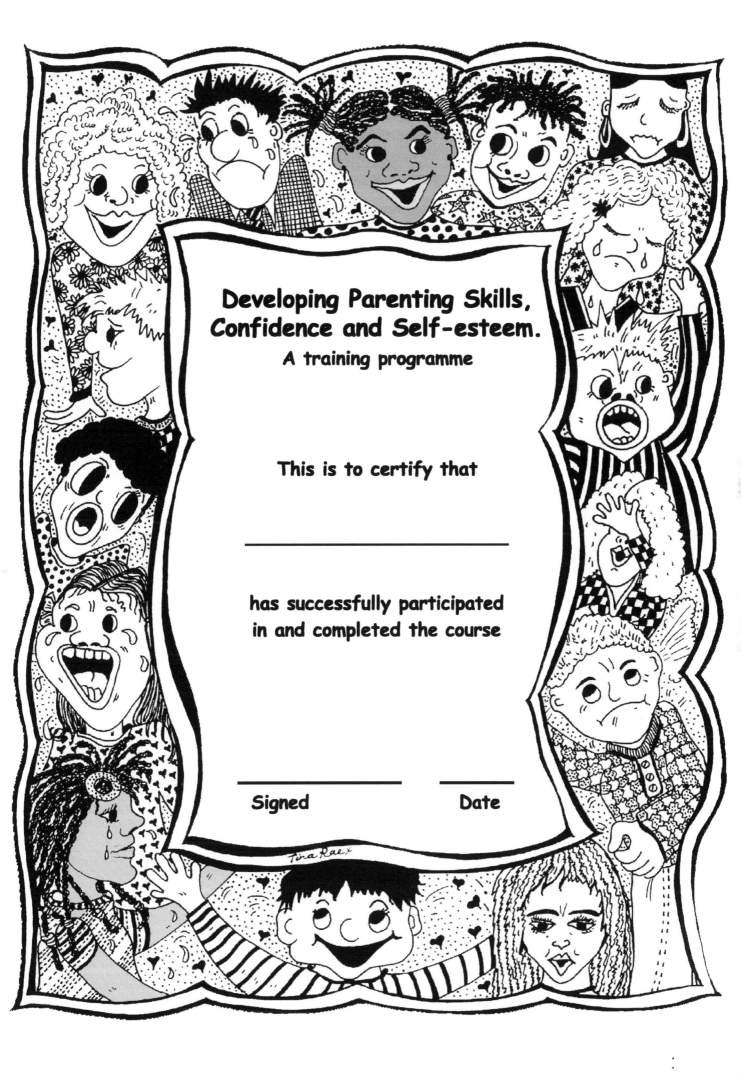

Developing Parenting Skills, Confidence and Self-esteem.
A training programme

This is to certify that

_____

**has successfully participated
in and completed the course**

_____   _____
Signed   **Date**

References

George, E., Iveson C. & Ratner H. (1990)
Problem to Solution: brief therapy with individuals and Families, London B.T. Press

Goleman, D. (1995)
Emotional Intelligence, New York: Bantam

Gottman, J. (1997)
The Heart of Parenting, London: Bloomsbury

Johnson, P. & Rae, T. (1999)
Crucial Skills, An Anger Management and Problem Solving Teaching Programme for High School Students, Lucky Duck Publishing

Lethem, J. (1994)
Moved to Tears, Moved to Action: solution focussed brief therapy with women and children, London B.T. Press

Miller, S. (1994)
Positive Parenting, Newcastle, Formword Ltd.

Mosely, J., & Gillibrand, E. (1995)
She Who Dares Wins Thorsans

Pugh G, De'Ath E & Smith (1994)
Confident Parents, Confident Children: Policy and Practice in Parent Education and Support National Children Bureau

Pugh, G. & Smith, C. (1996)
Learning to be a Parent, London: Family Policy Studies Centre

Quinn, M. & Quinn,T. (1987)
What can a parent do? Handbook for the 'fives to fifteens' programme, Family Caring Trust

Rae, T. (1998)
Dealing with Feeling, An emotional literacy curriculum, Lucky Duck Publishing

Rae, T. (2000)
Confidence, Assertiveness, Self-esteem, Lucky Duck Publishing

Rutter, M. (1991)
Pathways from children to adult life, Pastoral care in Education, Vol.9 No.3

Smith, C. (1996)
Developing Parenting Programmes, London: Routledge

Smith, C. (1997)
Developing Parenting Programmes, National Bureau Enterprises

Sutton, C. (1995)
Parent Training by Telephone, Behavioural and Cognitive Psychotherapy, 23, 1-24

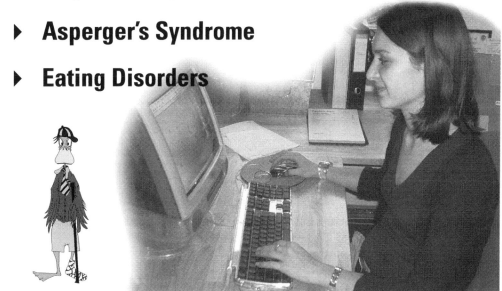